Clothing Decoration

By the Editors of Sunset Books

A

A. Soft, color-collaged knitted sweater has a shawl collar and is trimmed with crochet edging and belt. Design: Dione King. **B.** Felt-on-felt hand-appliquéd poppies, daisies, and forget-me-nots burst into bloom on this fitted vest. Design: Shari Smith.

Lane Publishing Co.
Menlo Park, California

B

Bouquets . . .

We would like to thank the following individuals and groups for their invaluable suggestions, advice, and support during the evolution of this book: Mark Adair, Clay and Fiber Gallery; Louise Allrich, Allrich Gallery; Beth Altschul, Levi Strauss and Company; Susan Boreman; Maggie Brosnan; Frances Butler; Darlene Carlson; Charles and Susan Clark; Robin Cleaver; Jean Cook; Mark, Christine, and Daniel Cragin; Dale Crawford, Kundus; Ruth Pearson Culbertson; Larry Dawson, Lowie Museum of Anthropology, Berkeley; Barbara DiConza; Molly Dimick; Connie and Wendy Earlez; Fiberworks, Berkeley; Eleanor Garcia; Andrea Gonsalves; Meredeth Grierson; Sandy Hagglund; Virginia Harvey, Costume and Textile Study Center, School of Home Economics, University of Washington, Seattle; Ellen Hauptli; Hope Hightower; Lilly Hillmer; Jean and Chris Isaacson; Gerhart Knodell; Marti Kortebein; Gyongy Laky; Lanna; Donna Osman Larsen; Nancy Lawton; Leslie Lievore; Mary Mashuta; Francis S. Merritt, Haystack School of Crafts; Michael Meyer; Inez Meyers, The Oakland Museum; Marsha Nygaard; Nance O'Banion; Nancy Papa; Peninsula Stitchery Guild; Libby Platus; Virginia Pribyl; Trudy Regan; Barbara Reid; Diane Ritch; Cindy Sägen; Sandra Sakata, Obiko; Julie Schafler, Julie Artisan's Gallery; Paul Smith, Museum of Contemporary Crafts; Sherrie Sullivan; Thousand Flowers, Inc.; Diana Turner, Portland Art Museum; Roberta Vandervort; Jerry and Anne Wainwright; Gwyneth and Natasha Warton; Lassie Wittman; Jackie Wollenberg; and personnel of the many museums and art galleries throughout the country who have been so very helpful.

Edited by Alyson Smith Gonsalves

Design: Tonya Carpenter
Artwork: Edith Allgood

Cover: Silkscreen decorated skirt and pinafore (see page 52). Skirt design: Jayne and Gary Lomax. Pinafore design: Vea Van Kessel. Photographed by Darrow Watt.

Editor, Sunset Books: David E. Clark

Second Printing November 1977

Contents

Special Features

Creative Clothing

Some of the most important things you own are the things that you wear on your back. Clothing is your home-away-from-home, your armor, your social talisman . . . or even a subtle message to kindred souls. In an instant, your manner of dress can suggest to the casual observer your selected age group, gender, social standing, and color preferences. Next to body language, the language of clothing is the most universal and timeless of all.

THE DESIRE TO DECORATE

Since time immemorial, garments have existed as functional work apparel or creations purely for the pleasure of the senses, as statements of financial and social or political standing, and (as the occasion demanded) as a method to attract the opposite sex.

Each purpose has its own set of recognizable visual symbols in the form of garment shape and, more commonly, garment decoration determined by the social mores of a specific culture. But what is acceptable to one society may be anathema to another; hence the delicious smorgasbörd of today's function and fashion.

Ethnic riches from every land now provide endless visual and sensual stimulation to anyone who wishes to partake, especially to individuals whose greatest pleasure is the embellishment of clothing in any way, shape, or form. The art of clothing decoration offers a means of expressing your own unique vision of the world, and sharing with others the resulting image of your Self.

COLORING YOUR WORLD

The ways and means of clothing decoration run the gamut from the use of leftover scraps and tools on hand to specially purchased paints, dyes, and brushes. You'll find as you page through this book that hundreds of ways exist for turning plain into fancy and for personalizing mass-produced, impersonal clothing.

Decorate the surface of your garment with beads, buttons, floss, appliqué, punchwork, patchwork, or one of the many other possible techniques; color the cloth itself with dyes, paints, or marking pens. Or refurbish the discards stuffed away in the back of your closet with crochet or knit work, piecing, machine embroidery, sewing and dyeing techniques, textile paints, scrap collages, or yarn drawings. We've included lots of large color photographs for you to use as project guides while you work.

We've also included a large number of "idea" photos and photo galleries (pages 40, 56, and 79) displaying the amazing applications and design work of professional clothing decorators to act as your own personal idea bank and study center. There's a lot to gain by evaluating the work of the pros in order to see how color, design, form, and function all come together into beautiful examples of clothing as art. Let their efforts spur you on to even greater achievements with your own decorative work.

COMMENTS ON CONTENT

To make things easy, we've applied most of our project ideas to simple, readily available classic clothing styles. These are garments you'll have little trouble purchasing ready-made or creating on your sewing machine.

For quick reference, decorative techniques are divided into chapters according to their application. Presented first is a section describing various kinds of surface decoration such as embroidery, appliqué, piecing, and

A. Strips of Seminole patchwork, shibori-dyed cloth, and bits of judiciously applied embroidery make this dress something very special. Design: Berta Bray.

B. Luxurious rayon chenille robe was worked in single crochet, passing color through color to achieve a sophisticated visual mixture; rows of "shells" edge cuffs and hem, while antler buttons act as closures. Design: Pamela Hinchcliffe.

C. Several cultures are combined in this special dress—molas from the San Blas Islands, ribbons from Europe, and know-how from California. Design: Yvonne Porcella.

D. Machine knitted, this simple, yet unusual sweater incorporates Japanese haiku poetry and calligraphic characters into its design. Design: Linda Mendelson.

E. "The Great Wave" washes across this beautifully color-blended man's knit pullover sweater. Design: Dione King.

braidwork. This is followed by a chapter concerning the use of dyes and fabric paints in techniques ranging from batik to silkscreening. And last, we discuss the gentle art of creative recycling, employing a variety of decorative applications.

Throughout these chapters are 40 pages of full-color photographs and illustrations to aid and inspire you as you work on individual projects.

If you have trouble finding certain materials, refer to page 78 for a list of suppliers. Books dealing with clothing decoration are also listed on page 78.

B

C

D

E

Basic Patterns to Decorate

Some garments lend themselves to embellishment more easily than others; those items that are simple in shape and timeless in their appeal are the best choices. Though either purchased or handmade clothing can benefit from the added zest and appeal of decorative work, the appearance of the garment you select has a lot to do with the success of the finished project.

Such classics as T-shirts, jeans and jeans jackets or skirts, work shirts, simple A-line or circle skirts, chef's aprons, classic sweaters, and ethnic-inspired clothing are all suited to decorative applications because each has a well-defined appearance and straightforward construction. Good sources for these garments include clothing stores, thrift shops, flea markets, and dime stores—or whip one up on your own sewing machine.

OFF THE RACK

When selecting likely candidates for decoration from ready-to-wear clothing, keep the following points in mind:

• Check for good construction and well-sewn seams so you won't be putting all your time and effort into decorating a poorly made piece of clothing that may quickly fall apart.

• Try to match the type of garment with the purpose you intend it to serve. For example, a casual jacket won't work as a dressy cover-up even if it *is* the perfect color. And color alone shouldn't determine your choice—consider the fabric weight and content of a garment as well.

• If you plan to use fabric dyes, select only garments made of natural fibers.

• The design of the clothing should be simple and uncomplicated; fussy detailing or intricate construction will compete visually with your workmanship.

By keeping these suggestions in mind as you shop, you'll avoid choosing the wrong type of garment for your needs.

BEING CREATIVE WITH COMMERCIAL PATTERNS

If you decide to make your own basic garment, select a commercial pattern with simple lines and as few pattern pieces as possible.

You can achieve the appearance of intricate construction yet keep the sewing simple if you cut large pattern pieces into smaller ones. When seam allowances have been added, these small pieces, in turn, can be used to cut out and repiece fabrics back into the original pattern shape that is then sewn to other pieces of the original pattern to complete the garment. For an example, see page 38.

Other alterations include interchanging individual pattern pieces from one pattern to another, altering the shape of a pattern piece to change its character, or creating a totally new design by combining the characteristics of several different patterns. The possibilities are really endless, and the changing parade of fashion makes new concepts in clothing construction readily available to the adventurous sewer.

ETHNIC CLOTHING'S GRAND TRADITION

While the word "ethnic" is most commonly used to identify the culture, customs, and language of particular segments of humanity, it also defines a classic type of garment structure—variations of which are indigenous to cultures in Mid-Europe, Africa, the Mediterranean, Asia, and the Far East.

Many of these garment patterns are today relatively unchanged in shape and style from their original design hundreds of years ago. This persistence of style is due to the absolute simplicity and appropriateness of these designs, which are based on the geometric shapes of the rectangle, square, triangle, and circle.

Patternmaking for and construction of ethnic clothing is very easy—each design is composed of a few simple pattern pieces with none of the mandatory open curves, darts, and other intricacies present in many currently available commercial patterns.

To give you an idea of the potential of these attractive, easy-to-make garments as foundations for a variety of decorative techniques, we've included eight basic patterns for ethnic garments, designed by Ellen Hauptli and Darlene Carlson. Each of these garments can be adjusted to fit women, men, or children. These ethnic patterns have been used for several of the decorative projects included in this book. Some examples appear on pages 25, 31, 39, 47, and 71.

The chart on page 10 shows you how to take the measurements needed to make the patterns; each of the eight designs lists the specific measurements necessary to construct that particular pattern. Basic mathematics is used to determine the dimensions of each pattern piece.

For example, the chest width of the Oriental dress pattern on page 13 reads $\frac{1}{4}$ F + 1″ to 2″. This means that if F equals 34″, you first divide 34″ by 4 to get $\frac{1}{4}$ F or 8½″. Then to 8½″ add an *ease* of 1″ to 2″ to get about 10″. This includes fabric for seam allowances; on other patterns, seams are marked ⅝″ or 1¼″.

MAKING ETHNIC PATTERNS

Keep a ruler, yardstick, French curve, scissors, tailor's chalk, and soft lead pencils on hand for patternmaking. A T-square is also useful for truing up the corners and edges of a pattern piece. Work on the floor or any other large flat surface where you can spread out your paper and tools.

To make patterns you'll need a large continuous roll of paper. Check with your local newspaper for newsprint end rolls. Wrapping paper rolls, usually carried by stationery or dime stores, and pattern drafting paper, generally found in fabric stores, are also adequate. Another good source for pattern paper is a medical supply house where you can buy the strong, flexible roll paper used on doctors' examining tables.

After each pattern has been cut out, check every individual pattern piece against the body of the person who will be wearing the garment to be sure that you have cut it correctly. Remember that these garments fit loosely over the body and that the pattern pieces may therefore be cut slightly larger than the comparable piece of a commercial pattern.

SPECIAL CONSTRUCTION HOW-TO'S

The basic shapes of ethnic patterns make them adaptable to a variety of necklines, hemming techniques, and closures. Directions and illustrations for these variations follow.

Necklines: Each neckline pattern can be made from a 10 by 15" rectangle of paper. Fold rectangle in half lengthwise, then fold it crosswise 4" down from the upper edge. Open up paper. The long fold indicates center fold of garment body; short fold is shoulder line. Center measurement I on shoulder line and mark. Also place a mark at intersection of the 2 folds. Measure back from this mark 1½" and mark. Paper should look like figure 7-A.

To make the various neck patterns, draw each of them as shown in figures 7-B, 7-C, and 7-D. Cut along this pencil line; remove paper from

neck opening and discard. There are 3 measurements for J; see measurement chart on page 10 for the right one to use for each neckline.

For the actual facing, cut a fabric rectangle 3" larger all around than neckline opening. Center and trace pattern on *wrong* side of facing fabric, using tailor's chalk or light pencil lines. Mark center point and shoulder line with pins on *wrong* side of facing and also on *right* side of garment (for a slit opening, draw a line 4" to 10" long down center front of facing *only*). Right sides together, pin facing to garment, checking for alignment.

Sew around neck opening on drawn line; for neck slit, sew ⅛" to either side and around base of straight line. Leaving a ½" seam allowance around neck, cut away both layers of excess fabric *inside* of sewn line. Clip curves, corners, and neck slit line, if present (fig. 7-E); then turn facing to wrong side and press. Check for fit and, if necessary, resew, adding ¼" *outside* of sewing line if neck opening is too small. (Make a new paper pattern later with correct opening size.) Turn under and sew any raw edges of facing. Topstitch ⅛" from neck edge to hold facing in place; then tack corners and edges of facing to wrong side of garment.

To face a neck opening with bias tape, mark neckline shape on wrong side of garment itself; then mark a second line ⅝" inside first line. Cut along second line and sew on bias tape, following package instructions.

A stand-up collar can be added to your garment, if you wish—just use a commercial collar pattern adjusted in

size to match the circumference of the garment's neck opening. Follow pattern directions to attach collar.

For a decorative effect, sew the *right* side of an extra-large facing to the *wrong* side of the garment, and then turn it to the *right* side of the garment after the neck opening has been cut, to make an attractive contrasting trim. The facing can be cut into a number of shapes, then appliquéd to the surface of the garment as shown in figures 8-A and 8-B.

Hems and finishing: The edges of cuffs and lower hems can be finished in several ways—turned and topstitched hems, commercial or homemade facings, bias tape bindings, cord and casing, tucks or pleats, and side vents—to vary the garment's look.

To turn and topstitch a hem, make two successive ¼" folds, individually pressing each fold. Topstitch close to top of first fold to secure (fig. 8-C).

Facings can be cut using the existing garment as your guide. Place a large extra piece of paper under the cuff or hem, then trace along its lower edge and 3" up both sides. Remove garment pattern and connect 3" lines with a line parallel to and 3" away from the lower edge line to complete facing pattern. Add ⅝" to each 3"-wide end of facing for seams, then cut out facing and press under ¼" along upper long edge. Folded right sides together, sew across short ends of facing. Next, right sides together, sew unfolded raw edge of facing to cuff or hem edge (fig. 8-D). Turn facing to inside and slipstitch (fig. 8-E) over folded edge to secure.

Cuffs and hems can also be finished

7-A

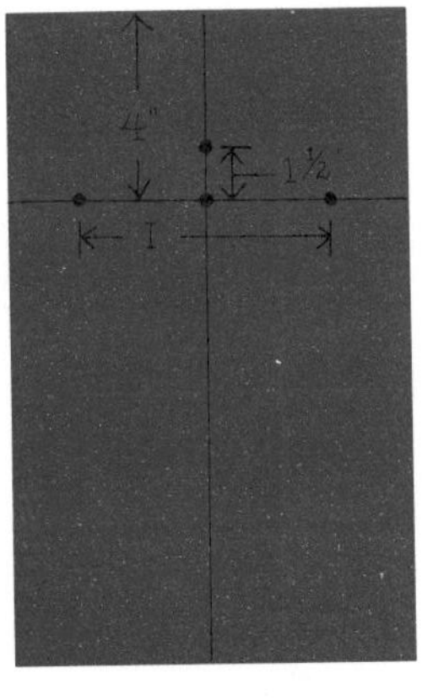

7-B

ROUND NECKLINE WITH SLIT

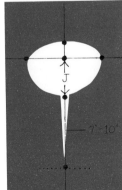

7-C

V-NECKLINE

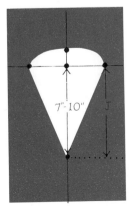

7-D

RECTANGULAR OR OVAL NECKLINE

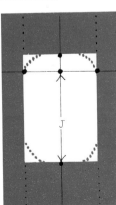

7-E

SEWING A FACING

GARMENT   FACING

CUT AWAY

with bias tape bindings. Trim seam to ¼" and cut a length of bias tape ½" longer than edge to be covered. Attach tape according to package directions, turning in ends of tape before second row of stitches (fig. 8-F). To make bias tape ties, cut bias strips at least 12" longer than edge to be covered. Open sleeve or side seam(s) about 2" and topstitch over raw edges of opened seam. Leaving 6" or more of tape free at each end, sew tape into place as for regular binding; complete by sewing along open edges and across turned ends of tape ties.

For a cord and casing finish, turn up or apply a 1" to 2"-deep hem or facing. Then open up sleeve or side seam *within* hem on outside of garment; sew across ends of open seam to prevent unraveling. Cut a length of cording 12" to 24" longer than length of casing, attach one end of cord to safety pin, and use pin to thread cording through casing. Remove pin and knot both cord ends (fig. 8-G).

A large sleeve may be tapered to the wrist by taking pleats or tucks. Before sewing up the sleeve, lay it out flat and decide on the number and placement of all pleats or tucks necessary to achieve the desired cuff size. Mark them with chalk; then fold and pin. For pleats, merely sew across bottom of folds to secure (fig. 8-H). For tucks, sew across bottom; then sew along edge of each pleat to tack it down completely (fig. 8-I). The sleeve can now be sewn.

Side vents are easy to do. After the side seams are sewn, but before the hem is turned up, put on the garment and decide how deep the vents should be. Mark side seams accordingly with pins; then remove garment and open seams to those points with a seam ripper. Tack across end of each side seam 3 or 4 times to keep it from opening further. Turn garment inside out and press under ⅛" along raw edges of the vent. Topstitch or slipstitch over fold (fig. 8-J).

Closures: Aside from buttons and buttonholes, here are a few suggestions for simple garment closures.

Cut even lengths of cording, each large enough when folded in half to pass over the button you plan to use plus 1" extra for seam allowance. Tack them in place along front opening of garment before seam is sewn;

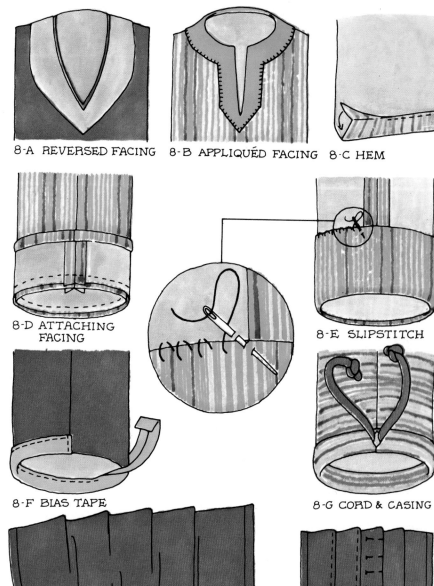

8-A REVERSED FACING

8-B APPLIQUÉD FACING

8-C HEM

8-D ATTACHING FACING

8-E SLIPSTITCH

8-F BIAS TAPE

8-G CORD & CASING

8-H SEWING IN PLEATS

8-I SEWING IN TUCKS

8-J SIDE VENTS

TACK

TOP STITCH

8-K CORD CLOSURES

CUT CORDS

CONTINUOUS CORDS

CORD TIES

8-L BUTTON LOOPS

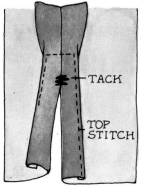

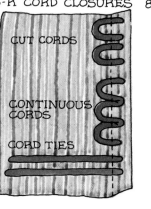

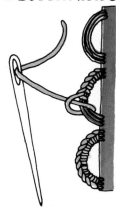

Basic Patterns to Decorate

Richly detailed, both the Mid-Eastern caftan and shirt (at right and below) have a centuries-old place in those cultures indigenous to northern Africa and the Mid-Eastern shores of the Mediterranean. Only three pattern pieces are needed to create either garment. Patterns are on page 11.

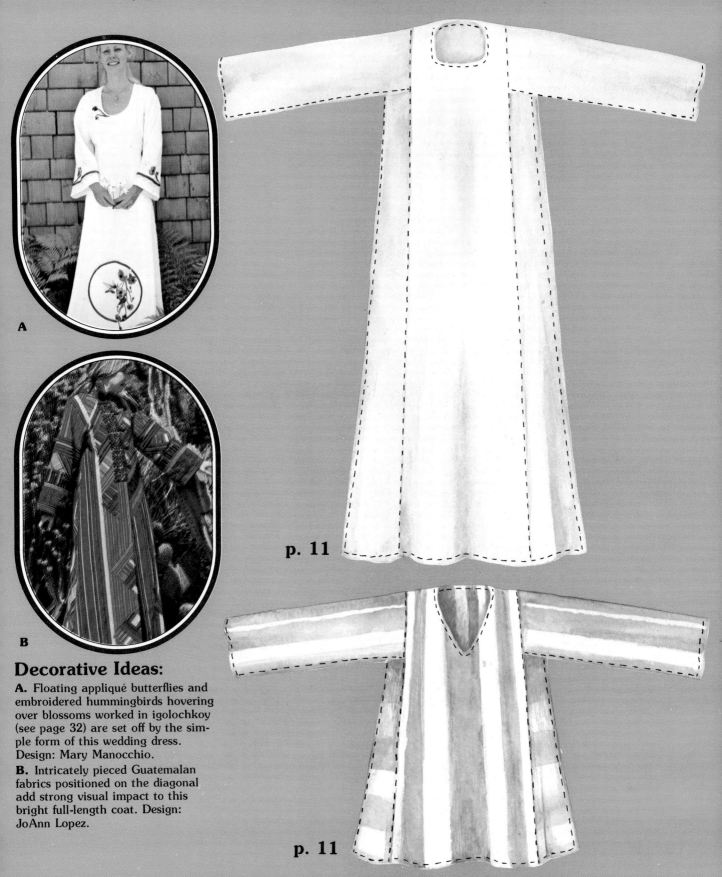

A

B

p. 11

p. 11

Decorative Ideas:

A. Floating appliqué butterflies and embroidered hummingbirds hovering over blossoms worked in igolochkoy (see page 32) are set off by the simple form of this wedding dress. Design: Mary Manocchio.

B. Intricately pieced Guatemalan fabrics positioned on the diagonal add strong visual impact to this bright full-length coat. Design: JoAnn Lopez.

then catch ends in seam as you sew down the front. Or use one continuous cord. Cord ties can also be sewn into the seam (all, fig. 8-K).

Button loops can be made by sewing several loops of doubled embroidery floss along the overlapping edge of the garment opening. Cover loops with buttonhole stitch, anchoring thread in lining (fig. 8-L).

YOUR PATTERN KEY

The chart shown at right indicates how and where to take body measurements if you intend to make any of the ethnic garments which follow; a key to the pattern illustrations is below.

Since yardage needs for all patterns will vary, depending on the size and length of the garment you're planning, take your pattern along when you buy fabric. Note: If imported or handwoven cloth is used, its high shrinkage rate means that extra fabric must be bought.

Before you start to sew, remember these pointers: See that the grain of your fabric is straight; then preshrink and press. If the pattern calls for folded fabric, fold it with wrong sides together on the lengthwise or crosswise grain; for unfolded fabric, lay fabric out right side up. Leave ⅝″ seam allowances except as otherwise noted. Baste with straight pins. Clip curves, corners, and seams as needed. Iron as you progress, pressing seams open unless otherwise indicated. For ease in matching pattern pieces, mark center front and center back of a pattern piece with pins.

PATTERN ILLUSTRATION KEY

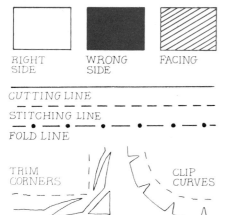

RIGHT SIDE   WRONG SIDE   FACING

CUTTING LINE

STITCHING LINE

FOLD LINE

TRIM CORNERS   CLIP CURVES

MEASUREMENTS KEY

Your Measurements:

_____ A: Center panel width—can be varied

_____ B: Hood depth—measure from base of neck to top center of head

_____ C: Armhole—keep tape loose around arm, enough to fit in 3 fingers

_____ D: Wrist—keep tape loose around wrist, enough for your hand to pass through

_____ E: Shoulder slope—use ruler held parallel to floor at base of neck

_____ F: Chest—measure at fullest width

_____ G: Waist—measure at natural waistline

_____ H: Hips—measure at fullest width (7″ to 9″ down from waist)

_____ I: Neck width—use ruler to measure neck base diameter, then add 1″ to 1½″ for ease

_____ J: Neck openings—measure down from I (neck width)

_____ K: Sleeve length—measure bent arm from neck vertebra to desired sleeve length

_____ L: Garment length—measure from top of shoulder to desired length

_____ M: Skirt length—measure from waist at center back to desired length

_____ N: Stride—take large stride, then measure from back heel to front toe (for adult: 35″ to 45″)

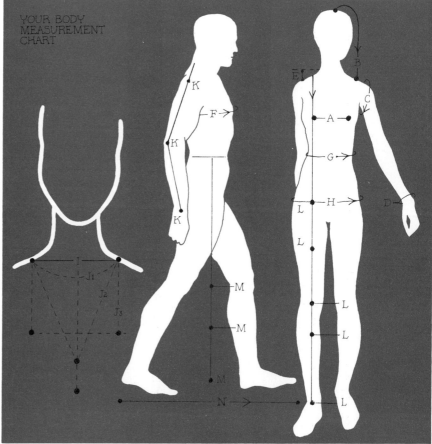

YOUR BODY MEASUREMENT CHART

Mid-Eastern Caftan and Shirt

COLOR ART ON PAGE 9

A true classic in our collection of ethnic patterns, the caftan described here can be interpreted in a number of ways: sleeves may be varied in shape and length; the garment can range from fingertip to ankle length; and the center panel can be as wide or as narrow as you wish. Decorated garments based on this pattern appear on pages 33, 34, and 39.

Note: Before purchasing fabric, please see "Your Pattern Key," page 10.

Measurements (see page 10): A, C, F, K, L, N for full-length caftan; A, C, F, H, K, L for shirt.

Caftan or shirt pattern: 1. For center panel pattern piece, cut a long rectangle of pattern paper measuring A + 1¼″ wide by 2 L + 1¼″ long (fig. 11-A).
2. To make sleeve pattern, cut a rectangle of pattern paper measuring C + 3″ to 9″ + 1¼″ wide by [K − ½ A] + 1¼″ long (fig. 11-A).
3. For side panel, cut a trapezoid from pattern paper measuring ¼[F + 2″ to 6″ − 2 A] + 1¼″ on top edge; ½[N − A] + 1¼″ on bottom edge for full-length or ¼[H + 3″ to 6″ − 2A] + 1¼″ on bottom edge for shirt; and L − ½[C + 3″ to 9″] + 1¼″ in length. As in figure 11-A, connect the 2 unmatched ends of trapezoid with a straight line to complete pattern piece.

Cutting: 1. Right side up, lay fabric out flat. Cut 1 center panel pattern.
2. Measure off enough fabric for 2 sleeves; fold fabric with right sides out, and pin sleeve pattern in place. Cut both sleeves at once.
3. Fold remaining fabric in half lengthwise and cut out 2 pairs of side panels (4 panels in all).
4. Remove pins and patterns; mark shoulder line of center panel and center folds of sleeves (fold from wrist to shoulder).

Caftan or shirt construction: 1. Add neckline of your choice (see page 7) and do any decorative work you desire while pieces are still flat.
2. As in figure 11-B, attach 2 side panels to each sleeve, leaving ⅝″ unsewn at underarm end of side panel seam.
3. Matching sleeve and shoulder folds, pin both sleeve/side panel sections to center panel, right sides facing. Sew from mark at shoulder fold to hemline front and back (fig. 11-C).
4. Right sides together, fold garment in half at shoulder marks, align all edges, and pin. Sew from underarm to wrist and from underarm to hem (fig. 11-D); then press seams open.
5. Turn up or face hems of sleeves and lower garment edge (see page 8).
6. To add more room for arm movement, a gusset may be inserted in underarm seam where sleeve meets center panel. Open underarm seam 4″ or more in both directions out from underarm and spread opening into a square shape. Underneath, place a square of fabric, which should extend 1″ beyond edges of opening. Pin gusset into place and topstitch close to edges of turned seam allowances. On the inside, turn under raw edges of gusset and sew down (fig. 11-E).

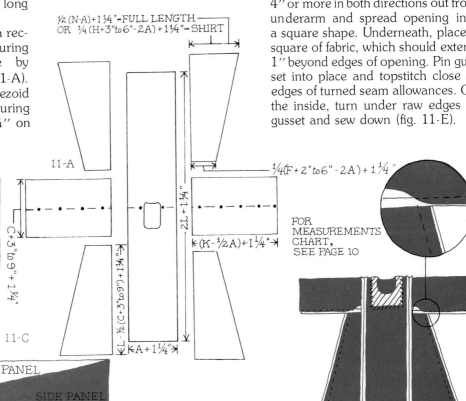

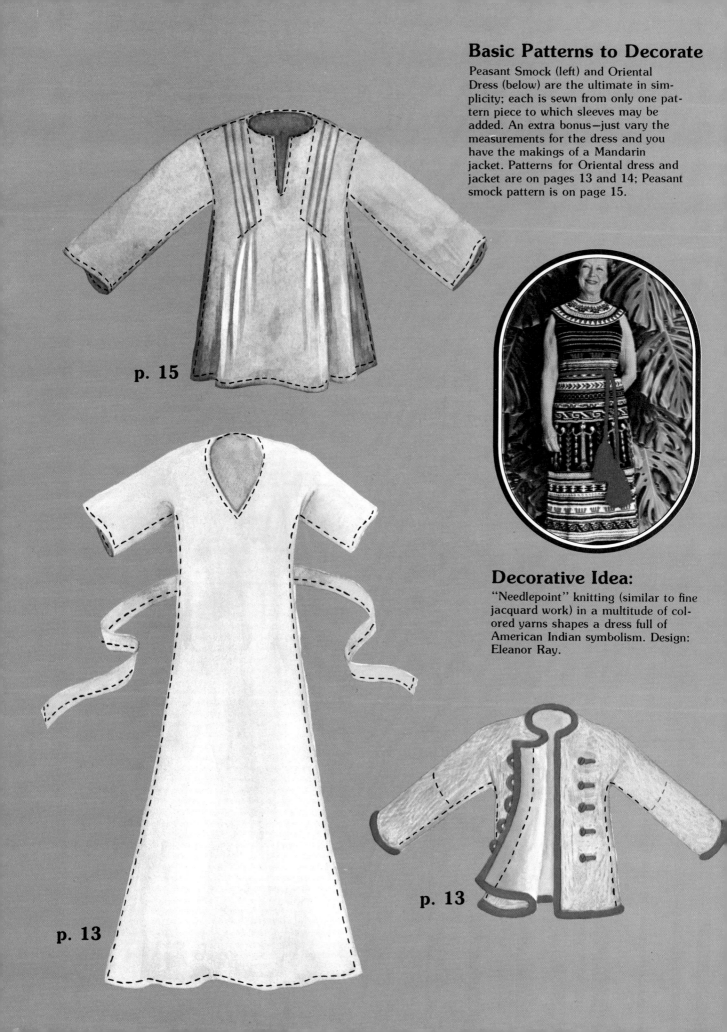

Basic Patterns to Decorate

Peasant Smock (left) and Oriental Dress (below) are the ultimate in simplicity; each is sewn from only one pattern piece to which sleeves may be added. An extra bonus—just vary the measurements for the dress and you have the makings of a Mandarin jacket. Patterns for Oriental dress and jacket are on pages 13 and 14; Peasant smock pattern is on page 15.

p. 15

Decorative Idea:

"Needlepoint" knitting (similar to fine jacquard work) in a multitude of colored yarns shapes a dress full of American Indian symbolism. Design: Eleanor Ray.

p. 13

p. 13

Oriental Dress and Jacket

COLOR ART ON PAGE 12

This simple one-piece oriental-style dress pattern is ideal for decorative techniques that must be applied before a garment is constructed. Since seams and shaping are at a minimum, the dress is especially suitable for batik, tie-dye, and silkscreen applications. An added attraction is its potential for variation. We've included instructions for converting the basic shape into an authentically styled Chinese side-opening coat.

Note: Before purchasing fabric, please see "Your Pattern Key," page 10.

Measurements (see page 10): C, D, F, K, L, and N for dress; C, D, F, H, K, and L for jacket.

Dress pattern: 1. Cut a piece of pattern paper measuring L + 3″ long by either [2 K] + 1¼″ or N + 1¼″ wide (use larger measurement). Fold this paper in half lengthwise to make 2 layers, each equal to L + 3″ by K + ⅝″ or [½ N] + ⅝″ (fig. 13-A).

2. Using figure 13-A as a guide, mark pattern as follows: point 1 (from top corner to hem: L + 3″); point 2 (length from top corner to cuff: K + ⅝″); point 3 (length from top corner to shoulder edge [¼ F] + 1″ to 2″); point 4 (length from point 3 on top of shoulder to underarm: [½ C] + 1″ to 2″); point 5 (from top of wrist edge straight down: [½ D] + ⅝″ seam, or use same measurements as in point 4 for wider sleeves); point 6 (from bottom center out to side seam: [½ N] + ⅝″). Measure 1 to 2″ above this last point and mark; then connect bottom center point to this mark with slightly curving line.

3. Connect points as follows: point 2 to point 5, point 5 to point 4, point 4 to point 6. Round off underarm angle for seam allowance; then cut out paper pattern. Finally, unfold pattern and indicate shoulder fold line.

Cutting: 1. Fold preshrunk fabric in half across grain, aligning top of paper pattern with folded edge of fabric; pin into place. (Note: It may be necessary to sew extra fabric onto selvages for long sleeves.) Cut out garment.

2. Remove paper pattern, unfold cloth, and mark shoulder line, then neck opening with tailor's chalk.

3. At this stage, garment is ready for preliminary decoration. To allow for easier decorative application, cutting of neck opening can be postponed until immediately before garment is assembled.

Dress construction: 1. Finish all preliminary surface decoration; then complete neck opening (see page 7). Pockets, if desired, may be added at this time.

2. To join side seams of garment, fold at shoulder line, right sides facing, and pin or baste all seams. Try garment on (inside out) and adjust for proper fit.

3. Sew both side seams and finish all raw seam edges. Clip underarm curves.

4. Turn garment right side out and try on. Check sleeve length and either turn under hem allowance or face sleeve edges with 1″ bias tape in a compatible color, following package instructions.

5. Measure lower hem and pin at correct height. Sew hem by hand or by machine.

Topstitching is optional but can be useful for anchoring facings at neck opening, sleeve edges, and hemline.

Jacket pattern: 1. To convert pattern for use in making a jacket, follow dress pattern steps 1 and 2, but change indicated measurements as follows (see fig. 14-A, page 14): point 1 (change to L + ⅝″); point 2 (retain K + ⅝″); point 3 (retain [¼ F] + 1″ to 2″); point 4 (change to [½ C] + 2″ to 4″); point 5 (change to [½ D] + 1″ to 5″ + ⅝″); point 6 (change to [¼ H] + 1½″ to 2½″ + ⅝″). Measure 1 to 2″ above this last point and mark; then connect center front of lower edge to mark with slightly curving line. Note that amounts added for ease in jacket pattern are greater than those indicated for dress—this allows room for jacket to be worn over other garments.

2. Connect points as for dress pattern. Round off underarm angle for ease; then cut out paper pattern. Finally, unfold pattern, indicate shoulder and center fold lines, and note that only 1 piece will be cut (fig. 14-B).

3. Cut pattern for front overlap of coat as follows: Prepare a piece of pattern paper L + ⅝″ long by ¼ H + 1¼″ to 2½″ + ⅝″ wide. Refold jacket pattern in half, place center fold on edge and mark its outline on overlap pattern paper (fig. 14-C). Mark a ⅝″ seam along right edge

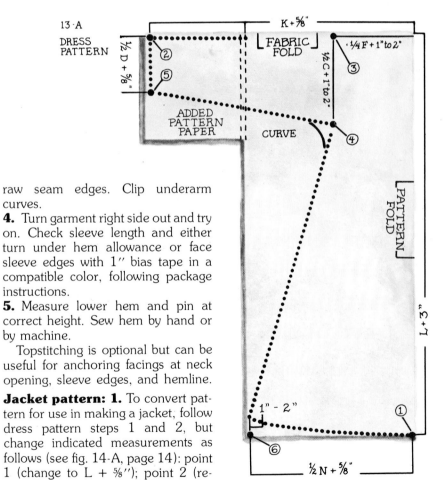

13·A

DRESS PATTERN

½ D + ⅝″

2

5

ADDED PATTERN PAPER

K + ⅝″

FABRIC FOLD

¼ F + 1″ to 2″

½ C + 1″ to 2″

3

CURVE

4

PATTERN FOLD

L + 3″

1″ - 2″

6

1

½ N + ⅝″

FOR MEASUREMENTS CHART, SEE PAGE 10

of overlap pattern; then draw in overlap, adding ⅝″ to outline for seam allowance. Overlap may take on a variety of shapes; a few examples are shown below. Select a style, draw it freehand onto pattern, add ⅝″ to outline, and cut out.

Cutting (follow these steps for cutting both outer jacket and jacket lining):

1. Fold preshrunk jacket fabric in half across grain, aligning top of paper pattern with folded edge of fabric; then determine amount of extra fabric needed for long sleeves. Cut these extra pieces and sew on as in figure 14-D. Refold pieced fabric; then reposition and pin pattern. Cut out jacket. Repeat for lining.

2. Remove paper pattern, unfold cloth, and very accurately mark shoulder line and front center line on material with tailor's chalk.

3. Draw in chosen neck shape with chalk (see page 7) and add ⅝″ seam allowance inside of this line.

4. Carefully cut jacket front opening and inside line of neck along chalk lines (fig. 14-E).

Jacket construction: 1. Pin front overlap pattern to remaining jacket fabric and cut out overlap. Right sides together, sew overlap to left front cut edge of jacket opening, carefully aligning lower edges. Press seam open; then cut away flap point at neckline to align with the cut neck edge (fig. 14-E). Repeat for lining.

2. Right side *up*, lay jacket out flat. Right side *down*, place lining over jacket fabric and align edges. If a collar or binding is desired, see page 7. Pin together and stitch as indicated by dotted lines in figure 14-F. *Do not sew* underarm sleeve and side seams. Turn right side out and press.

3. Fold garment in half at shoulder line with lining to inside. Stitch underarm and side seams with ¼″ seam allowance. Trim away seam allowance close to stitching and clip underarm curves.

4. Turn jacket inside out and press all seams. To finish seams, lay jacket flat and stitch through both layers of jacket ⅜″ in from sleeve and side seams. This leaves a finished edge on both inside and outside of garment, making it reversible.

5. Refer to page 8 for information on adding closures.

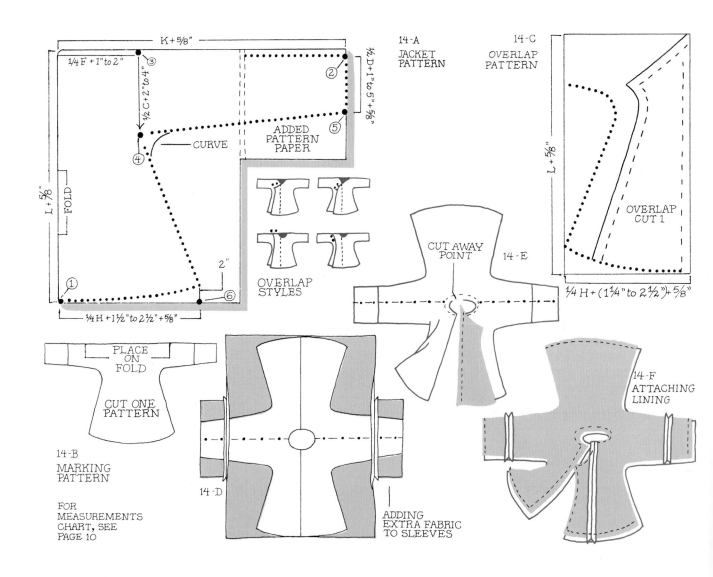

K + ⅝″

¼ F + 1″ to 2″

½ C + 2″ to 4″

CURVE

L + ⅝″

FOLD

2″

¼ H + 1½″ to 2½″ + ⅝″

½ D + 1″ to 5″ + ⅝″

ADDED PATTERN PAPER

14-A JACKET PATTERN

OVERLAP STYLES

CUT AWAY POINT

14-E

14-C OVERLAP PATTERN

L + ⅝″

OVERLAP CUT 1

¼ H + (1¼″ to 2½″) + ⅝″

PLACE ON FOLD

CUT ONE PATTERN

14-B MARKING PATTERN

FOR MEASUREMENTS CHART, SEE PAGE 10

14-D

ADDING EXTRA FABRIC TO SLEEVES

14-F ATTACHING LINING

European Peasant Smock

COLOR ART ON PAGE 12

Based on a simple rectangular pattern, this smock takes its shape from the use of well-placed tucks. These can be positioned and sewn in such a way as to give the smock either a tailored or a loose fit. Sleeves may be added or, if you wish, the smock can remain sleeveless and double as an overblouse.

Note: Before purchasing fabric, please see "Your Pattern Key," page 10.

Measurements (see page 10): C, E, F, K, L.

Smock pattern: 1. To make smock body, cut a rectangle of pattern paper measuring $2L + 4''$ long by $\frac{1}{2} F + 13\frac{1}{4}''$ wide. (The $13\frac{1}{4}''$ addition covers tucks, shoulder overhang, ease, and seam allowances.)

2. For sleeves, cut a paper rectangle $[C + 1'' \text{ to } 3''] - 2E + 1\frac{1}{4}''$ wide by $K - [\frac{1}{4} F + 3''] + 1\frac{1}{4}''$ long.

Cutting: 1. Right side up, lay fabric out flat and cut 1 smock body piece. **2.** Fold remaining fabric in half with right sides out. Pin sleeve pattern in place and cut both sleeves at once.

Smock construction: 1. Center and mark neckline (see page 7) on wrong side of smock.

2. Following figure 15-A, mark off tucks in this manner: Fold smock in half lengthwise and mark center line with pins. Open up smock and lay out flat, right side up. Mark garment with pins $2\frac{1}{2}''$ out from center line on either side. Also place pins at points $5\frac{1}{4}''$ in from each of garment's outer edges. This defines area in which tucks should be made. Remove pins from center line, then mark and pin 1 parallel line between and equidistant from the other 2 lines of pins. Mark all 3 pin lines with tailor's chalk; then remove pins to make 3 tuck lines.

3. To make tucks, which appear on face of garment (when sewn with fabric right side up), or can be hidden on inside (when sewn with fabric wrong side up), take up fabric and fold along each chalk line; pin along folds from front to back (fig. 15-B). The longer the tucks, the more fitted the smock; conversely, the shorter the tucks, the looser the smock.

4. Sew tucks $\frac{1}{2}''$ from fold to ends of markings as in figure 15-C. Ends of tucks can be left free after pressing, or seam for last inside tuck can be extended diagonally to the outside to seal ends of all tucks (fig. 15-D).

5. Right sides together, fold garment in half at shoulder line. Mark off measurement E at each outside shoulder edge; then from both edges draw a line from E to just inside edge of neckline marking. Sew these shoulder darts from neck out to shoulder. Press darts open and flat (fig. 15-E). Re-mark neck opening if necessary for smooth lines.

6. Face neck opening as marked on smock (see page 7), remembering to adjust facing to fit shoulder dart slope.

7. Refold garment as in step 5. From outside edge of each shoulder, measure and mark a line $\frac{1}{2} C + 1''$ to $3''$ long running down to a point $2''$ in from each side seam of smock. Then draw diagonal lines from these points back out to smock's lower corners (fig. 15-E). Pin garment sides along these lines; try on smock and adjust for correct fit; then cut away excess fabric $\frac{5}{8}''$ outside markings.

8. If *no* sleeves are wanted, sew side seams to point where line turns to angle back to shoulder edge. Press seams open. Hem or face edges of armholes and lower edge (see page 7 for suggestions).

9. If sleeves are desired, skip Step 8. Align sleeves with smock at shoulder line and, right sides facing, pin and sew them into place, leaving $\frac{5}{8}''$ unsewn at each end of shoulder seam.

10. Right sides facing, fold garment in half at shoulder line. Align and pin edges. Sew from underarm to bottom hem; then sew from underarm to wrist edge. Clip. Press seams open. Hem or face sleeve edges and bottom hem.

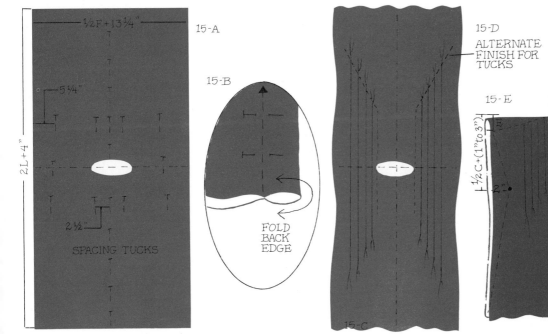

Traditional Ethnic Treasures

Visual delights can emerge from any culture—witness the collection displayed here. These authentic embellishments are the glory of many ethnic cultures. Come and explore the gems of this international treasure-trove.

A. Dahomey, Africa: Appliqué fish is a traditional pattern representing the last great Dahomean king, Behanzin (1889–1892).

B. Rajastan palace slippers from India were worked in brightly colored, definitive embroidery designs against a dark ground.

C. Heavily applied embroidery and braidwork create panels of color on this fringed Serbian garment.

D. Adinkara cloth, from the Ashanti tribe of Africa, uses indigo dye applied by hand stamps fashioned from heavy gourds.

E. The richly embroidered designs of this Dalmatian dress show the influence of a number of other Mid-Eastern cultures.

F. Kuskokwin River Eskimo sealskin boot displays bead trim, plaited wool ties, and appliquéd dyed-leather strips.

G. Diornede Island rain parka, pieced together from strips of walrus gut, is impervious to snow or sea water. Brown fur tufts and puffin topknots act as trim.

H. Traditional costume of Russian "Old Believer" features bright igolochkoy designs.

I. Incredible hand embroidery of this pre-1850 antique Chinese robe is worked predominantly with satin stitch accented with areas of bound stitch.

J. Ukrainian cross-stitch shirt alternates stitched panels with lace insets.

K. Detail of an appliqué panel from Gujerat, India, showing commonly used overall floral and serrated patterns.

L. This pair of tiny, delicately embroidered slippers was designed for the bound feet of a high-born Chinese lady.

M. Strong geometric pattern of ikat-dyed Japanese kimono results from the exact interlocking of predyed warp and weft threads.

A

B
C

E F

D

N. Strips of ribbonlike Seminole Indian patchwork being readied for use.

O. Yugoslavian woman's felt vest bears chainstitch embroidery, pompons, and a wealth of very heavy lace trim.

P. San Blas Island mola is finely worked in reverse appliqué, a technique in which layers of colored cloth are stacked, cut through to the desired color, and then sewn down around the edges to create an overall design.

A, D, K, N, and **P** courtesy of Cindy Sagen; **B, C, E, J, L,** and **O** courtesy of the Costume and Textile Study Center, School of Home Economics, University of Washington; **F** and **G** courtesy of the Lowie Museum of Anthropology, University of California, Berkeley; **H** courtesy of Jean Cook; **I** courtesy of 1000 Flowers, San Francisco; **M** courtesy of Fiberworks, Berkeley.

G

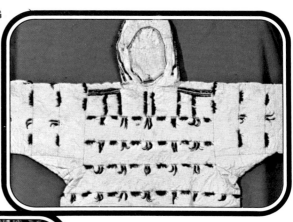

H

I

J

L

M

K

N

O

P

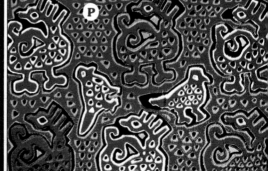

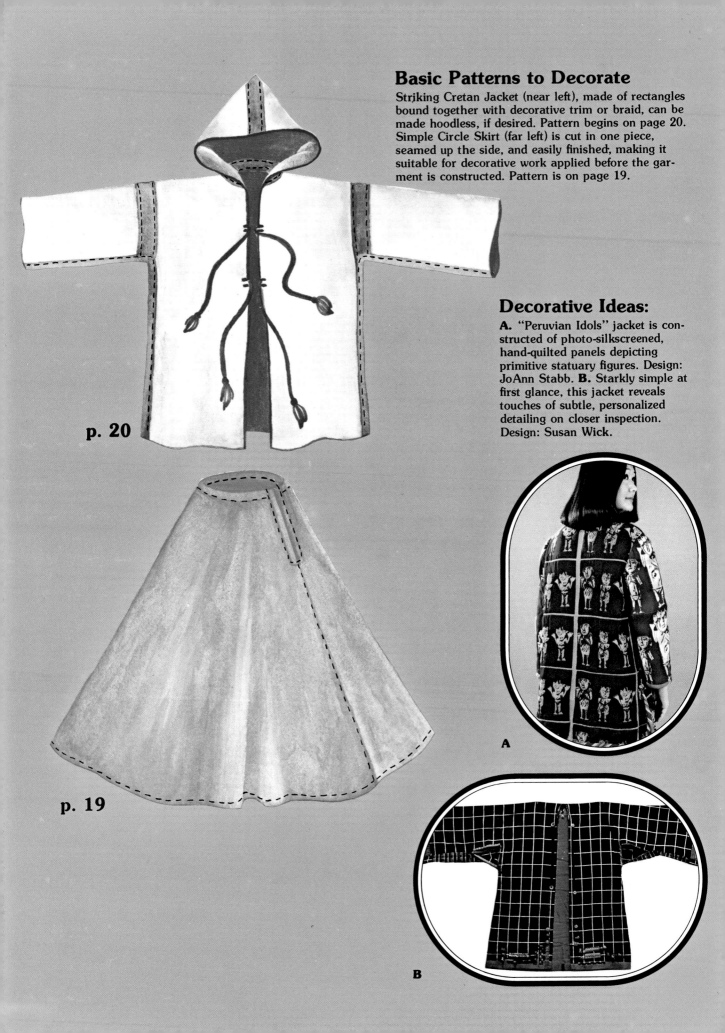

Basic Patterns to Decorate

Striking Cretan Jacket (near left), made of rectangles bound together with decorative trim or braid, can be made hoodless, if desired. Pattern begins on page 20. Simple Circle Skirt (far left) is cut in one piece, seamed up the side, and easily finished, making it suitable for decorative work applied before the garment is constructed. Pattern is on page 19.

p. 20

p. 19

Decorative Ideas:

A. "Peruvian Idols" jacket is constructed of photo-silkscreened, hand-quilted panels depicting primitive statuary figures. Design: JoAnn Stabb. **B.** Starkly simple at first glance, this jacket reveals touches of subtle, personalized detailing on closer inspection. Design: Susan Wick.

A

B

Simple Circle Skirt

COLOR ART ON PAGE 18

Simple to make and great to wear, this easy semicircle skirt is cut in one piece and finished with a bound waist, a sewn side seam with a short zipper, and a turned or topstitched hem. Its classic styling will suit just about any purpose, depending on the type fabric used. Light to medium-weight woven fabrics are best, but even knits can be used if they aren't too stretchy.

You'll also need a ball of string, a tack, and a pencil to fashion a large-radius compass, and a 7-inch skirt zipper, 1 packet of ½''-wide twill tape, and 1 packet 1''-wide bias seam binding (if you plan to turn the hem).

Note: Before purchasing fabric, please see "Your Pattern Key," page 10.

Measurements (see page 10): G, M.

Skirt pattern: 1. Cut a square of pattern paper equal to M + 1'' by M + 1''. Piece paper if necessary to achieve a large enough square. Mark 1 edge "fold" and 1 adjacent edge "selvage."

2. Cut a length of string equal to ½ G + ⅝''. Following figure 19-A, curve string in a quarter-circle shape slightly below inner corner of pattern where edge marked "fold" meets edge marked "selvage" until both ends of string just touch pattern edges at equal distances from inner corner. Mark touch points and remove string.

3. Improvise a compass by tying a length of string to a pencil and using a tack to secure string in place at inner corner. Holding pencil upright and keeping string radius taut, mark a curved dotted line from touch point to touch point (fig. 19-B). This is the waist *seam* line.

4. Waistline is very important at this point. Check again and make necessary adjustments. Shorten compass string slightly; then measure and mark a solid line ⅝'' inside dotted line to indicate waist *cutting* line.

5. To mark skirt length, measure M + 1'' down from waist seam line on both fold and selvage edges of pattern and at intervals between them (19-C); place pencil marks at these points. Using improvised compass, extend string radius from inner corner to pencil marks and draw a quarter circle from pencil mark to pencil mark. Cut out skirt pattern.

Cutting: 1. Iron out center (long) fold of preshrunk fabric; then refold cloth in half across length.

2. Lay paper pattern over folded fabric with waist at a corner where fold and selvage meet. If pattern is too wide for folded cloth, sew an extra strip of fabric to 1 selvage of cloth and readjust center fold accordingly.

3. Pin pattern into place and cut out skirt. Remove pattern.

4. Lay skirt out flat and mark all seam lines. Also place a mark 7⅝'' down from skirt waistline on selvages.

Skirt construction: 1. Cut a length of twill tape ½'' longer than waist measurement. Pin tape to *wrong* side of waistline. Sew into place along seam line (fig. 19-D).

2. Right sides together, align selvage edges and pin. Start at waist and machine baste selvage edges together, stopping at a point 7⅝'' down from waist edge. Backstitch. Switch to normal stitch length and sew to skirt hem. Press seam open.

3. Insert skirt zipper according to package instructions.

4. Bind waist edge of skirt with bias tape (fig. 19-E); handstitch tape around zipper. Add hook and eye, if desired.

5. Pin skirt to a hanger by waistband and allow to hang for 4 days to give areas cut on the bias time to stretch.

6. Try on skirt and re-mark stretched areas. Trim along bottom edges of skirt to even the hemline.

7. Overcast hem edge or finish with bias seam binding.

8. Turn up hem and baste.

9. Blind hem or topstitch hem. Press with steam iron to set hem crease.

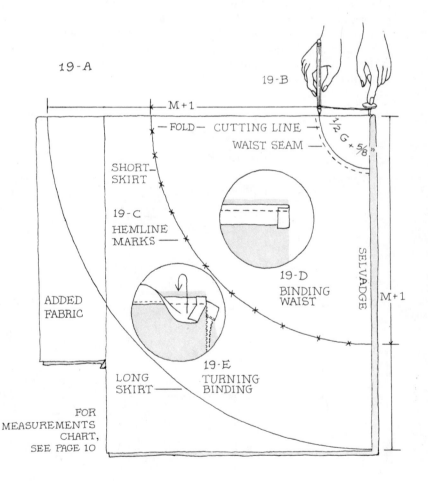

19-A
19-B
M + 1
FOLD — CUTTING LINE
WAIST SEAM
½ G + ⅝''
SHORT SKIRT
19-C HEMLINE MARKS
19-D BINDING WAIST
SELVADGE
M + 1
ADDED FABRIC
LONG SKIRT
19-E TURNING BINDING
FOR MEASUREMENTS CHART, SEE PAGE 10

Cretan Island Jacket

COLOR ART ON PAGE 18

If you want a garment pattern that adapts to many different applications, try the Cretan Island jacket pattern described here. It is a modular piece of clothing made from four fabric rectangles of varying sizes joined with braid, trim, or hand-crocheted edging. The jacket can be made from light, medium, or heavy fabric, depending on the degree of warmth desired. Remember, though, that very heavy fabric will give you bulky seams.

Note: Before purchasing fabric, please see "Your Pattern Key," page 10.

Unless you plan to have the finished garment drycleaned, preshrink all fabric and trims. A variation of this pattern appears on page 71.

Besides the jacket fabric you'll need fabric for jacket lining (same amount as for jacket), pattern paper, yardstick, pencil, pins, and chalk. To finish the jacket you'll also need braid or trim (to determine the amount needed, measure along all edges to be joined by trim and add 12 inches), a ball of worsted knitting yarn in a matching or contrasting color, and a large-eye tapestry needle.

Measurements (see page 10): B, C, F or H (use the larger of these two measurements), I, K, L.

Jacket pattern: 1. To make pattern for jacket body, cut from pattern paper a rectangle measuring 2 L + 1¼" long by ½ (H or F—use larger measurement) + 3" to 4" + 1¼" wide.
2. For sleeve pattern, cut a rectangle of paper that measures K − ¼ (H or F) + 1¼" long by C + 4" to 8" + 1¼" in width.
3. For hood pattern, cut a paper rectangle measuring 2 B + 4" to 8" + 1¼" long by 2 I + 1¼" wide.

Cutting: 1. Pin jacket pattern to jacket fabric and cut out 1 jacket body. Unpin and use pattern again to cut 1 jacket body from lining.
2. Cut 2 sleeves simultaneously from jacket fabric folded with wrong sides together. Repeat for sleeve linings.
3. For hood, pin pattern to jacket fabric and cut 1 hood pattern piece.

Unpin pattern and reuse to cut 1 hood piece from lining fabric.
4. Remove paper pattern from jacket body and lining. Fold both fabrics across their widths to find shoulder lines; mark these lines with chalk. Indicate neck opening on wrong side of lining fabric by centering measurement I on shoulder line and marking both ends of I. Next, find and mark center point of I and center point of front bottom edge of jacket body. Connect these 2 points to mark front jacket opening (fig. 20-A).
5. Find and mark lengthwise center folds of sleeves and sleeve linings.
6. If pockets are desired, make and add them at this time. The easiest pockets to make are square patch pockets. Cut 7⅝" by 7⅝" squares of both jacket fabric and lining. Pin fabric squares to lining squares, right sides facing, and sew as in figure 20-B. Turn pockets right side out and slipstitch along open edge (see page 8, fig. 8-E). Press pockets flat.

Pin pockets into place on front of jacket body fabric and topstitch ⅛" in from edge along sides and bottom.

Jacket construction: 1. Right sides together, pin jacket body, sleeves, and hood each to their respective linings. Sew as in figure

FOR MEASUREMENTS CHART, SEE PAGE 10

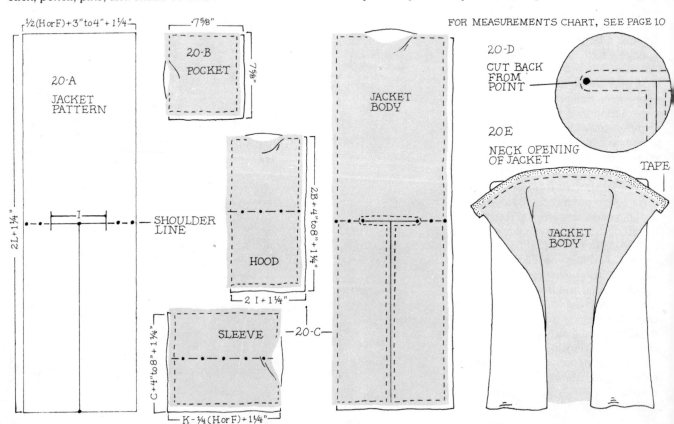

20-C. Clip corners; then cut between lines of stitching for jacket opening and neckline. Trim neck (fig. 20-D).

2. Turn all pieces right side out and press seams flat. Slipstitch along all openings to close (see page 8).

3. To join hood to jacket body, first cut a piece of trim equal to circumference of neck opening plus 1¼″. Lay opening out flat. Leaving ⅝″ excess trim at each edge of neck opening, lap trim ¼″ over *outside* of neck edge and pin in place (fig. 20-E). Topstitch along overlap, close to edge of trim. Pin free edge of attached trim to hood, matching hood ends to neck opening ends and overlapping trim ¼″ on outside of hood (fig. 21-A). Topstitch along overlap, close to edge of trim. Fold ⅝″ of excess trim at each neck edge to inside of hood and sew down by hand. Whipstitch top edges of hood together (fig. 21-B).

Cut piece of trim measuring length of hood seam + 1¼″. Fold under ⅝″ at 1 end and, starting at front of hood, whipstitch trim over exposed seam. At the back, fold tape into a V-point (fig. 21-C) before sewing it down; complete attachment of trim.

4. Attach right sleeve to jacket body with trim cut to a size exactly equal to sleeve width. Pin trim to sleeve as for trim attachment to jacket body in step 3. Topstitch along overlap, close to edge of trim. Match shoulder lines of jacket body and right sleeve. Attach sleeve to jacket body as for hood attachment to jacket body in step 3. Repeat entire step to attach left sleeve.

5. Join sleeve seams and sides of jacket by cutting 2 lengths of trim, each equal to length of sleeve + length from underarm to lower edge of jacket body + 1¼″ excess. Set 1 length of trim aside.

Leaving ⅝″ excess trim at lower edge of jacket body, lap trim ¼″ over outside of body edge and pin into place. Work up body edge, pinning trim in place, continuing around underarm angle and ending with ⅝″ excess trim left at cuff edge of sleeve.

Topstitch along overlap, close to edge of trim (fig. 21-D). Pin free edge of attached trim to back edges of sleeve and jacket body. Overlap trim ¼″ on outside of back edges. Topstitch along overlap, close to edge of trim. Fold ⅝″ of excess trim at cuff edge and at lower edge to inside and sew down by hand. Repeat with re-

maining trim for 2nd jacket side seam.

6. For decorative stitched edging, embroider blanket stitch (fig. 21-E) along all edges of jacket using woolen worsted yarn and tapestry needle. Space stitches about ½″ apart.

7. To make braided tie closures (see page 18): for each tie cut three 2-yard lengths of yarn and fold 2 lengths together at middle to form a group of 4 lengths. Thread 3rd length of yarn onto a needle and attach to jacket as in figure 21-F. Before pulling loop tight, thread 2 ends of the group of 4 lengths through it and position their midpoints at center of loop. Pull loop tight to secure.

Divide this group of 6 ends into 3 groups of 2 ends each. Now braid the 3 groups together until you have a braid 8″ long. Temporarily set braid aside. For tassel, cut thirteen 8″ lengths of yarn and hold 12 of them together as 1 group. Divide braid into 2 groups of 3 ends each and tie a firm knot around middle of bundle of 8″ yarn lengths. Double over bundle; then wrap and knot remaining 8″ length around doubled over bundle ½″ from braid. Trim ends of tassel (tassel may also be made for hood).

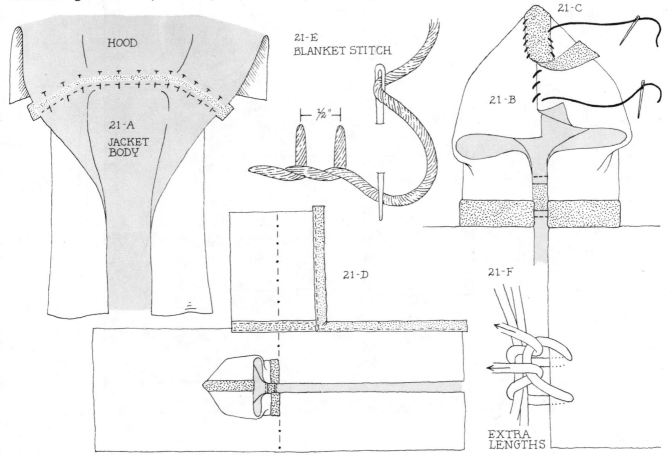

21-E
BLANKET STITCH

½″

HOOD

21-A
JACKET
BODY

21-D

21-C

21-B

21-F

EXTRA
LENGTHS

French Chef's Apron

COLOR ART ON PAGE 23

At right is an original version of the professional French chef's apron. This design is a true culinary classic that is both serviceable and decorative. Made of sturdy blue or white cotton fabric, the apron is perfectly flat before the pocket is attached, so all sorts of decorative techniques may be applied. For one design idea, see page 49.

An adult size apron requires 1¼ yards of fabric, 3 yards of cotton cording, and two 24″ lengths of bias tape.

Measurements (see illustration 22-A below): Those used for a man's apron are indicated with an (m); those for a woman's apron with a (w); and those for a child's apron with a (c).

Apron pattern: 1. Cut a rectangle of paper to fit dimensions of apron size you've chosen (i.e., 30 by 32″ for a woman's apron).

2. Fold long sides of pattern in half to find center of apron. Then open pattern out and center neck measurement (10″ for a woman's apron) on fold and mark each end of neck.

3. Measure down 8″ from these marks and draw a line parallel to neck line completely across pattern.

4. Connect neck marks to pencil line below and use a plate or saucer to draw in underarm curves (fig. 22-B). Cut out pattern.

5. Pocket is a rectangle of fabric measuring 9 by 20″ for an adult's apron, and 7½″ by 17″ for a child's apron.

Cutting: 1. Lay patterns out flat on grain of fabric and pin in place. Cut out fabric and unpin pattern.

Apron construction: 1. Turn all edges under; then hem all except underarms, where a bias tape channel is sewn for neck and tie cord. Leave ends of channels open to allow cord to slip through. Run cording through channels, even it up, and knot both ends.

2. Turn under all 4 edges of pocket and hem; then center pocket on apron (5″ below underarm for adults; 3 to 4″ for a child), pin it in place, and stitch around each section as shown in figure 22-C. For extra strength, make 2 rows of stitching. Narrow pocket channel in the middle measures 4″ wide and keeps pocket flat.

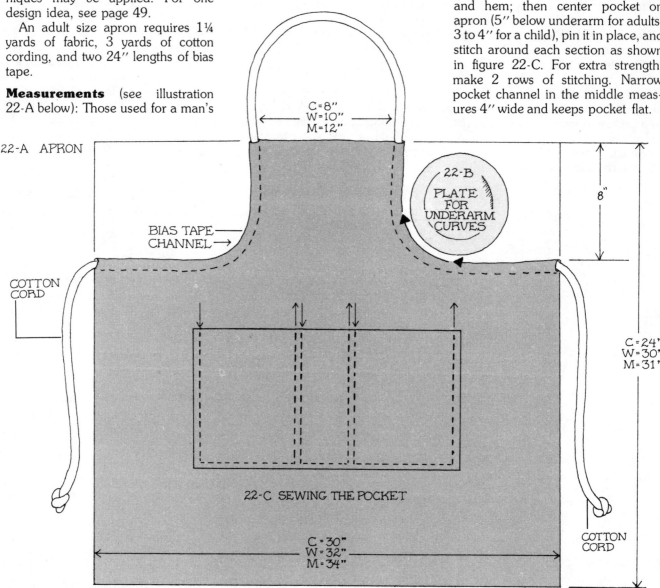

22-A APRON

C=8″
W=10″
M=12″

22-B PLATE FOR UNDERARM CURVES

8″

BIAS TAPE CHANNEL →

COTTON CORD

C=24″
W=30″
M=31″

22-C SEWING THE POCKET

COTTON CORD

C=30″
W=32″
M=34″

Basic Patterns to Decorate

Simple and straightforward, the classic French chef's apron is ideally suited to many decorative techniques. The apron itself can be of almost any material or color, and its flat shape adapts well to surface or dye decoration. The pattern begins on page 22.

Decorative Ideas:

A. The apron as tunic: Patchwork, embroidery, and enameled decorations carry this apron into the realm of fantasy. Design: Nancy Welch.
B. Short apron transformed: This full-length hostess apron sports handworked farmland appliqués. Design: Margaret Stuermer.

p. 22

A

B

Surface Decoration

It's easy to see that the most popular single approach worldwide to the enhancement of garments is that of surface decoration. Quilting, embroidery, patchwork, and appliqué have long been favored internationally as ways in which to embellish an article of clothing—but have you considered variations on these traditional approaches as well as some of the fascinating, less widely known means of surface decoration? Read on.

THE ETHNIC ROOT

Most established approaches to surface decoration have evolved because of our strong ethnic heritage of needlecrafts. Each technique has its own special look and feel, yet the possible variations on the basic themes run into the hundreds, since each culture has its own interpretation of how a needle can be used to best advantage.

Because we live in an age when the availability of such ideas coincides with the existence of enough leisure time to develop and master the techniques involved, we are in a uniquely favored position; all forms of self-expression are open to us if we want to reach out and take them.

TECHNIQUES TO TRY

One way to start is to sample the small but select collection of surface decoration ideas we've assembled on the following pages. Develop a taste for Russian punchwork, American Indian Seminole patchwork, and Danish *slentre* braiding. Or create an all-American embroidered sampler work shirt. Learn to love your sewing machine for the ease and speed it can lend to your decorating efforts, not to mention the interesting results possible only with machine work. Get involved with trims, floral embroidery, or strip patchwork. All in all, we think you'll find the journey most enjoyable. But first a word about basics.

MATERIAL MATTERS

Another phenomenon peculiar to today is the wide availability of crafts materials from various parts of the world. Extensive importing of fabrics, trims, yarns, threads, and small craft equipment has made access to exotic materials and tools a reality. Large cities boast numerous outlets for crafts materials, while individuals living in relatively isolated areas can make use of various craft mail-order services. (A short list of mail-order supplies appears on page 78.)

Fabrics used for our projects consist of natural fibers or blends; easy to work with, they have the right "feel," both tactilely and visually, for hand decorated clothing. It is a good idea, though, to preshrink everything you use—even blends—to keep your work from "puckering up" the first time it's washed or dry-cleaned. This is especially important when imported or handwoven cloth will be used, because the shrinkage rate is generally high; be sure to buy extra fabric to make up for the amount lost.

For a strong, long-lasting support or backing for your surface work, choose firmly woven fabric; it will hold up far better than fine, delicate fabrics.

Trims can add unique touches to appliqué and patchwork endeavors; just be sure they are well-made, first-quality trims. These, like fabrics, require preshrinking, especially if they're made from natural fiber materials.

Yarns and threads are also available in profusion; both domestic and imported varieties offer many exciting possibilities for self-expression. For our projects we've tried to use yarns, cords, and threads that are widely available; but don't feel limited to only our choices. If you want to substitute a favorite yarn, cord, or thread for a specific material, just be sure to make appropriate adjustments in the pattern if your selection is different in size from the original materials specified in a pattern.

Special threads for machine embroidery are now available in a wide range of colors and materials from a number of sources. This thread is constructed differently from sewing thread and will cover your design area better than regular thread. If you aren't able to locate it, just use regular cotton sewing or quilting thread instead.

Cotton and rayon flosses have been used for embroidery projects. These are widely available in dime stores, yarn shops, fabric stores, and many other outlets. If you use cotton floss, preshrink it first since it will shrink up after sewing when it is washed for the first time.

Small craft equipment, such as needles, embroidery hoops, latch hooks, crochet hooks, and knitting needles, is usually available in fabric or yarn shops. Other specialty equipment can be mail ordered from the suppliers listed on page 78.

TRANSFERRING PATTERNS

The designs in this book are bordered by evenly spaced dots. To use them, first make a grid of squares over the design by connecting the dots with horizontal and vertical lines.

To enlarge the design, use the grid size indicated on the pattern to create on your pattern paper a larger grid composed of squares equaling the indicated grid size. Copy the original pattern, one square at a time, onto the larger grid to achieve a full-size pattern. Use dressmaker's carbon, or transfer pencils and tracing paper to transfer your design to your fabric. Remember—transfer pencil markings are permanent, so apply them carefully. To avoid smudging transfer lines, don't move the dry iron; press straight down and hold till transfer takes.

Surface Decoration

Curving band of Seminole patchwork (far left) is applied to our circle skirt pattern (see page 19). Directions are on page 27. Design: Lynn Blackwell. Hand-embroidered floral bouquet graces a purchased denim skirt (below, right). Directions are on page 26. Design: Robin Wagman.

Idea:

Hand-embroidered fantasy world peopled with wildly colored flora and fauna wraps completely around this classic denim jacket. Design: Anna Polesny.

Embroidered Floral Skirt

COLOR PHOTO ON PAGE 25

Faded denim makes a dramatic backdrop for the embroidered floral fantasy highlighted here. The bouquet includes poppies, anemones, and lilies whose texture and color changes result from 14 assorted tints worked in 8 different embroidery stitches (given below).

You'll need: 1 skein cotton embroidery floss in *each* of the following number-coded colors: light green (1), medium green (2), dark green (3), medium orange (4), dark orange (5), gold (6), light pink (7), medium pink (8), dark pink (9), pale coral (10), deep coral (11), brick red (12), medium lavender (13), and dark lavender (14); crewel embroidery needle; medium-size embroidery hoop; scissors; iron; denim skirt.

1. Enlarge and transfer design below to lower front of skirt (see page 24).
2. Divide all colors of floss (except for half of gold floss) into 2-strand segments. All embroidery on this skirt is worked in 2-strand floss, except all gold French knots which are worked with 6-strand floss.
3. Fit skirt into hoop. Start working from center of design and continue outward, changing position of hoop as necessary to keep work area centered. Progress either from 1 color to another, or from 1 stitch to another, following the color number codes and stitch symbols below. Colors and stitches are drawn in full color on the floral pattern.
4. When finished, lightly steam press embroidery face down on a padded ironing board.
5. Always launder this skirt by hand in warm water.

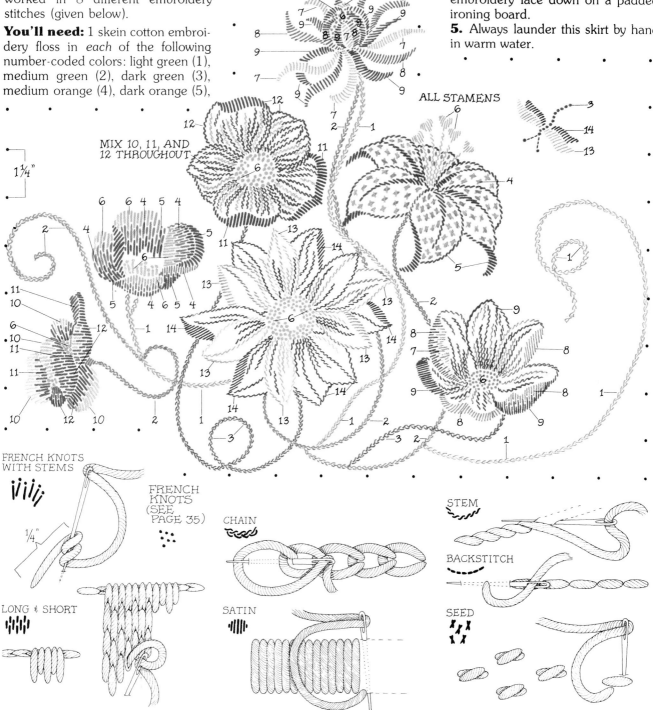

MIX 10, 11, AND 12 THROUGHOUT

ALL STAMENS

FRENCH KNOTS WITH STEMS

FRENCH KNOTS (SEE PAGE 35)

CHAIN

STEM

BACKSTITCH

LONG & SHORT

SATIN

SEED

Seminole Patch Skirt

COLOR PHOTO ON PAGE 25

Originated by Florida's Seminole Indians, this patchwork technique was first employed in the 18th century to brighten the drab calico yardage traded to the Indians by Spanish settlers. Much less complex to make than it appears, Seminole patchwork consists of long, narrow strips of fabric sewn together and then cut crosswise into bands of equal size. The bands are then resewn in an offset placement, creating a diagonal design (see below).

For best effect, all fabric used for patchwork should be of uniform weight and texture; avoid knits or other stretchy materials. Keep visual confusion to a minimum by limiting yourself at first to only three or four colors or patterns which separate well from one another. Braid, ribbon, and rickrack, if used with discretion, make lively accents when positioned between strips of brightly colored fabric.

Most Seminole patchwork strips are evenly trimmed and sewn together on their long edges to form a larger fabric with an overall patched surface design. Our project, though, makes use of a single row of patchwork applied to a skirt made from the circle skirt pattern on page 19.

To achieve the effect of row upon row of patchwork, sew Seminole patch strips together along their length, stitching just inside the zigzag edge. Trim off points and iron strips out flat. Continue to add rows of patchwork until your pieced fabric is the desired size.

You'll need: 5 yards of 1½″-wide loop-edged navy blue satin ribbon; 7½ yards yellow piping; cotton fabric in the following amounts and colors: ¼ yard 45″-wide red polka dot, ¼ yard 45″-wide yellow print, ¼ yard 45″-wide red and white striped, and ½ yard 45″-wide fuchsia; 1 yard fusible webbing; scissors; straight pins; pencil; circle skirt.

1. Cut 1½″-wide and 45″-long strips in the following amounts and colors: 6 fuchsia, 3 red polka dot, 3 yellow print, and 3 red and white striped. Also cut six 45″ lengths of yellow piping and three 45″ lengths of navy blue ribbon. Fold each piece of navy ribbon in half lengthwise and crease; cut along crease to divide each into 2 strips of ribbon, making 6 ribbons in all.

2. Using ¼″ seams, sew each half-strip of navy ribbon to a 45″ length of fuchsia fabric (fig. 27-A), forming six 2-strip sections.

3. Right sides facing, sew a strip of red polka dot fabric to each ribbon edge of 3 of the six 2-strip sections. Repeat for striped fabric strips and remaining three 2-strip sections.

4. Right sides facing, sew yellow piping along both edges of each strip of yellow print fabric; use a zipper foot to sew as close to piping as possible.

5. Again using zipper foot, sew the 3-piece strips of fuchsia—navy ribbon—polka dot fabric to one edge of each of the piped yellow print fabric strips, right sides together. Repeat for remaining 3-piece strips of fuchsia—navy ribbon—striped fabric. Press all seams toward centers of completed pieces (fig. 27-B) which should measure about 5½″ wide by 45″ long.

6. Using 2 of the 3 pieced strips, cut each into fifteen 3″-wide pieces. Cut four 3″-wide pieces from third strip and set remainder aside.

7. Divide pieces into 2 groups of 17 pieces each; then join each group of pieces as in figure 27-C, offsetting each color strip by one fabric row and leaving ⅛″ unsewn at beginning and end of each seam. Iron all seams to one side. This will give you two 42″-long bands of offset patchwork.

8. Iron under all raw edges of fuchsia fabric and navy ribbon; then lay patchwork bands over fusible webbing and cut webbing to fit size and shape of each band.

9. To attach bands to skirt, lay skirt out flat with single side seam at center front. With pins, measure and mark points falling 20″ down from waistband at each edge of skirt. Position 1 piece of webbing and its matching patchwork band across skirt from edge to edge, lining up top edges with pins. Following directions for applying webbing, fuse patchwork band to skirt. Topstitch along all edges to secure.

10. Repeat step 9 to attach second band to other side of skirt.

11. Cut out two 6 by 6″ squares of fuchsia fabric and iron under ¼″ on all sides of each square. Position and line up each square to cover and match raw ends of each patchwork band; pin and sew squares into place with topstitching. Measure off enough navy ribbon to reach from both navy strips of one band end around angle of square to navy strips of adjacent band end. Fold ribbon to same width as ribbon used in patches; then iron these lengths of ribbon in half lengthwise and topstitch into place as in figure 27-D. Repeat for remaining band ends and fuchsia square.

27-A

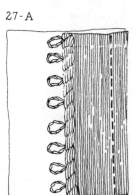

27-B

27-C

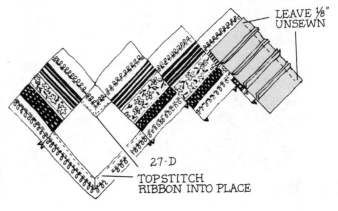

LEAVE ⅛″ UNSEWN

27-D

TOPSTITCH RIBBON INTO PLACE

Machine Embroidered Smock

COLOR PHOTO ON PAGE 31

The pretty pastel floral bouquets presented here add a spritely touch to our peasant smock pattern (see page 15). To apply this machine embroidery design to the finished garment, you'll need only an inexpensive embroidery hoop and several spools of machine embroidery thread.

To start, clean and oil your machine; then lower or cover the feed dogs (check your machine manual for specifics for your particular machine). If the feed dogs do not need to be lowered or covered, set stitch length to 0. Remove the all-purpose presser foot; then either use an embroidery foot or, if your machine does not have one, just remove the presser foot screw. Remove the needle and put in a size 11 or size 70 needle.

Set top thread tension at 0 or −; top tension must be loose so that the bobbin thread doesn't show on the right side of the fabric. Ensure invisibility by checking the bobbin tension and tightening it if necessary.

Fill the bobbin with machine embroidery thread (the color doesn't matter since it won't show on the surface of the fabric). Thread the machine with machine embroidery thread and set stitch width at medium. *Note:* As you work, readjust the width to suit the design.

For practice, select a large scrap of homespun and place the fabric *right* side up over the larger ring of the embroidery hoop; then press the smaller ring down on the fabric inside of the large hoop. Pull fabric taut.

Now draw lines, curves, spirals, and zigzags on the fabric with pencil, and slip the hoop under the needle. Lower the presser foot bar, which triggers both thread tensioners. Bring the lower thread to the surface of the taut cloth, and begin to stitch. Work slowly, moving the hoop back and forth or from side to side.

When stitches run across pencil lines, you're doing a satin stitch (good for outlines or monogramming); when the stitching runs parallel to the line, you're sewing the side stitch (used for filling in large areas).

Fill in areas by moving the hoop slowly from side to side, blending and overlapping stitches. Try to fill in objects following their shapes; work floral shapes in a circular motion, avoiding rows of stitches.

You'll need: 1 spool of #50 machine embroidery thread in *each* of the following colors: light blue, dark blue, light peach, dark peach, light purple, dark purple, light yellow, gold, light green, medium green, dark green, and brown; unhemmed and unfaced smock (see page 15) of white homespun; tissue paper; pencil; transfer pencil; iron; scissors; zigzag sewing machine; 1 size 11 or size 70 machine needle; a 6″ or 8″-diameter embroidery hoop.

1. Enlarge and trace embroidery designs below (see page 24) onto tissue paper with transfer pencil. To make mirror-image tracings of designs, lay tissue paper tracing face *down* over white typing paper and retrace design from back with transfer pencil onto another sheet of tracing paper.

2. Position shoulder embroidery pattern 1½″ in from raw sleeve edge and centered on shoulder seam. Iron on transfer according to transfer instructions. Repeat for other shoulder area.

3. Position hemline corner embroidery 3″ up from raw hem edge and 1½″ in from raw side seams. Iron on transfer. Repeat for second corner.

4. Embroider designs in this order, following individual shapes and changing width of zigzag to conform with size of area being filled in: Work leaves first, filling them in from center vein, working outward to edges. Sew veins and stems in side stitch after leaves are filled in.

Next, go to single-color flowers, filling in with a circular motion using center as axis. For centers, set zigzag at 1 and use a small, circular motion.

Go on to two-toned flowers, doing the outside (usually lighter) shade of petals first. Follow by filling in darker central area and end by stitching in yellow centers as for smaller flowers.

Finish by embroidering butterflies. Work from wing edges inward, doing bodies last. Work antennae with zigzag set at 1, and stitch length at 0.

5. Finish sleeves and hem of smock as described on page 15.

★ ALL LEAF VEINS ARE DARK GREEN

★ ALL FLOWER CENTERS ARE GOLD UNLESS OTHERWISE NOTED

¾″

1″

⊞	LIGHT BLUE
⊞	DARK BLUE
▦	LIGHT PEACH
▨	DARK PEACH
⊡	LIGHT PURPLE
▥	DARK PURPLE
▥	LIGHT YELLOW
▭	GOLD
▥	LIGHT GREEN
▥	MEDIUM GREEN
▭	DARK GREEN
▬	BROWN

Dolly Appliqué Smock

COLOR PHOTO ON PAGE 31

Doll up a smock for your daughter with this cheerful machine appliquéd design. The doll is pieced together with fusible webbing and machine zigzag satin stitching, and then bonded and stitched to the smock. Hand embroidery is employed for facial features and dress detailing.

The pattern below can also be used to make a freestanding doll: Just combine the head and body patterns and add ½ inch all around to the new pattern. Do all detail work first; then cut out 2 matching pieces and sew with a ¼-inch seam. Turn and stuff.

You'll need: ¼ yard of 45″-wide homespun cotton fabric or large fabric scraps in the following colors: buff, burnt orange, turquoise, and dark brown; ½ yard fusible webbing; 1 spool brown and 1 spool turquoise sewing thread; brown, turquoise, black, and orange embroidery floss; embroidery needle; small amount of batting or fiberfill; zigzag sewing machine; pins; scissors; pencil; typewriter paper; girl's smock made from blue cotton fabric (see page 15).

1. Enlarge pattern to correct size and transfer individual patterns to typewriter paper as follows: 1 body pattern (buff), 2 cuff patterns (brown), 1 apron pattern (burnt orange—note: cut away scalloped center), 1 bodice pattern (blue), 1 belt pattern (brown), individual patterns for skirt appliqués (blue), fringe patterns for bottom of apron (blue and brown), 1 face pattern (buff), and 1 hair pattern (brown).

2. Use patterns to cut out corresponding parts of design from preshrunk fabric in colors designated in step 1. Don't allow for seam allowances because edges of these pieces will all be overcast with machine zigzag satin stitching.

3. For each part of design (except for doll's face) cut a slightly smaller corresponding piece of fusible webbing. Position and fuse individual fabric pieces (according to package directions for bonding) to buff body shape in the following order: blue bodice, brown cuffs, burnt orange apron, brown belt, blue and brown fringes, and blue apron designs. Bond hair to head with scraps of bonding.

4. When all pieces have been fused to head and body, apply zigzag satin stitching over all raw edges of fabric pieces, except for outside edges of body and head. Use blue thread for all blue appliqués, brown thread for all other appliqués.

5. Add embroidery floss details to dress and face as indicated on pattern. Illustrations for running, French, satin, and stem stitches are below.

6. Center doll body and its piece of fusible webbing on lower front of smock, keeping bottom of doll about 2½″ up from turned hem. Fuse body to smock.

7. Fuse head and hair to smock, slightly overlapping body, with bonding corresponding to shape of hair; this leaves face and chin free. Stuff a small amount of batting or fiberfill into head; then zigzag over chin area with brown thread to close.

8. Complete by zigzagging over all raw edges with brown thread.

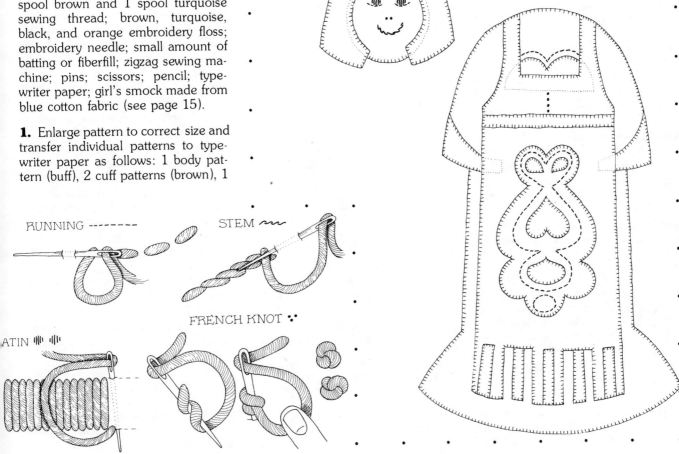

RUNNING

STEM

FRENCH KNOT

SATIN

HAIR OVERLAP

⌐ 1¼″ ⌐

Braid-bordered Shirt

COLOR PHOTO ON PAGE 31

If you like braids or plaited trims, you'll like this easy approach to making your own in record time—and having fun doing it. This braid, though native to a number of cultures, takes its name from Scandinavian sources. It is called *slentre*, which means ''to saunter or stroll'' in Danish.

Here's how it works: a warp of five individual looped cords is knotted over a hook at one end and held at the other end by the fingers of both hands; the fingers pass the loops back and forth between hands, in effect ''walking'' them to and fro to form a length of beautiful braid very similar to that used for French epaulets.

We've used slentre here to add a touch of opulence to a man's Mid-Eastern shirt (see page 31). Two variations of slentre are used on this shirt—one variation (solid color) is made from five lengths of maroon crochet cotton; the other uses four strands of orange perle cotton, combined with three or five strands of maroon crochet cotton which are held and worked as though they were one.

You'll need: One 115-yd. ball of maroon mercerized crochet cotton 8-cord cable twist (or equivalent); two 27.3-yd. skeins of orange perle cotton; scissors; yardstick; 1 spool maroon thread; needle; white glue; finished man's shirt in burnt orange made from pattern given on page 11.

1. To start 1 length of basic slentre braid, cut five 72″ lengths of maroon crochet cotton. Fold lengths in half and gather all cut ends into one knot to make 5 looped working lengths of cord. Attach knot to a solidly anchored hook or nail. Using *only* second, third, and fourth fingers of both hands, put your fingers *down* through loops as shown in figure 30-A.

To start the braid, hold cords taut; then use finger 2 of left hand to reach through loop held by finger 3 of right

hand and pull loop off of finger 4 right hand back through finger loop 3 right and over to finger 2 of left hand. Now move loop held by finger 3 of right hand to finger 4 of right hand and move loop held by finger 2 of right hand to finger 3 of right hand. To tighten braid, pull hands out to sides and keep cords taut. You have now completed 1 cord pass (fig. 30-B).

For second and final cord pass, use finger 2 of right hand (which is now

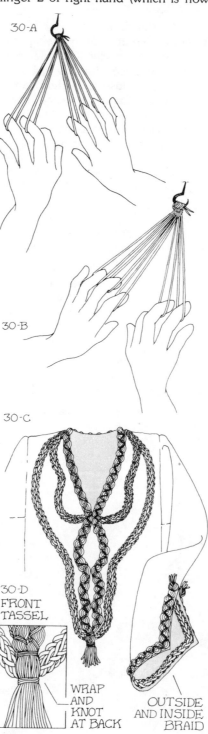

30-A

30-B

30-C

30-D
FRONT
TASSEL

WRAP
AND
KNOT
AT BACK

OUTSIDE
AND INSIDE
BRAID

free) to reach *through* loop held by finger 3 of left hand and pull loop off of finger 4 of left hand back through finger loop 3 left and over to finger 2 of right hand. Now move loop held by finger 3 of left hand to finger 4 of left hand and move loop held by finger 2 of left hand to finger 3 of left hand. Tighten braid as before.

You have now completed one step of the braid; your fingers should be holding cord loops as in figure 30-A. Continue to alternate in this way, passing cords back and forth from right to left and left to right until you have only enough room left to finish off loop ends of 5 working cords into a single knot. You have now completed one entire braid.

2. Following step 1, make 3 all-maroon slentre braids from 72″ lengths of cord, and 2 all-maroon slentre braids from 60″ lengths of cord. Set all braids aside.

3. To make 1 two-color neck braid, cut four 72″ lengths of orange perle cotton and five 72″ lengths of maroon crochet cotton. Fold and knot all cords as in step 1 and put knot on hook. Now hold all 5 maroon cord loops on *one* finger and work as though this group were 1 cord. Use other cords as in step 1. This braid has a serpentine appearance.

Repeat this entire step to make remaining neck braid; then make 2 matching cuff braids using 60″ lengths of cord, but cutting and working with only 3 maroon cords held as 1, instead of 5 as for neck braids.

4. When all braids are completed, pin neck braids in place as shown in figure 30-C. Cut off knots at *one* end of each maroon braid and glue. When dry, cover cut ends of maroon braids with two-color neck braids. At lower center front, bring the 4 braid ends together and wrap them into a single large tassel (fig. 30-D). Join two-color neck braids at back of neck into a tassel in the same manner.

5. Pin 1 two-color braid to outside edge of each cuff; knot braid ends. Cover hem at inside of each cuff with a single maroon braid pinned into place. Trim off cord ends and apply white glue to prevent raveling.

6. To sew down braids, use maroon thread and work just under both edges of braid using slipstitch (see page 8, fig. 8-E).

Surface Decoration

Machine embroidered bouquet (below, left) was created on our Peasant Smock (see page 15), as was the charming doll appliqué (below, center). Directions for embroidery and appliqué are on pages 28 and 29, respectively. Embroidery design: Hilde Lee. Appliqué design: Phyllis Dunstan. Our Mid-Eastern Shirt (far right—see also page 11) sports French epaulet-braid trim. Directions for Braid-Bordered Shirt are on page 30. Design: Jackie Wollenberg.

Idea:

Amazingly intricate detailing in embroidery and appliqué on this jacket depicts the goings-on of a family of whimsical mice. Design: Belva Long.

Punchwork Caftan

COLOR PHOTO ON PAGE 33

Russian punchwork—or igoloch-koy (*ee-go*-luch-koy) as it is traditionally called—is a beautiful but little-known 17th century handcraft.

Practiced by the "Old Believers"—a small religious community that originally left Russia in the 17th century to escape religious persecution—this simple art of creating a fine, intricate plush design with a tiny handmade needle was long practiced only within the confines of isolated "Old Believer" communities.

Now, though, the tool needed for igolochkoy is being made available to outsiders. Easy, dramatic, and inexpensive, igolochkoy is sure to gain great popularity. For equipment information, see page 78.

1. Cut out individual fabric pattern pieces as described on page 11, drawing (but not cutting out) neck opening on *wrong* side of main fabric pattern piece.
2. Trace 4 copies of bird #1, 5 copies of bird #2, and 1 copy of bird #3 with yellow transfer pencil onto tissue paper. Lay main fabric pattern

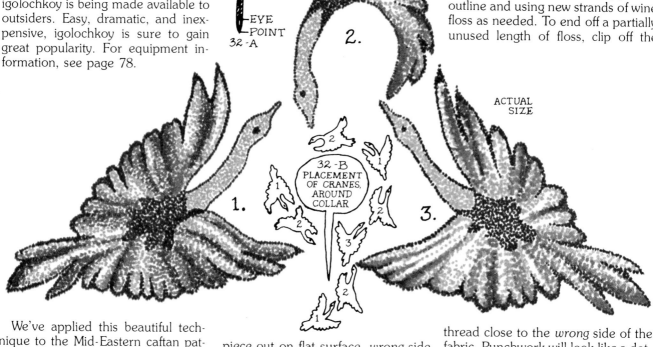

it enters needle shaft. To pull thread through needle, suck hard on hollow needle point with your mouth; thread will slip through. Finally, thread 2″ at end of strand out through needle's eye. Needle is now ready.

4. Working with *wrong* side of fabric up, center 1 crane design in embroidery hoop and pull fabric taut. Begin your punchwork by outlining bird in this manner: Holding needle like a pencil (at a 45° angle) and trailing thread over the back of your hand, start at base of crane's neck. Punch through to other side of fabric until plastic sleeve of needle touches fabric surface. Still holding needle at an angle, withdraw needle until it rests on fabric surface (don't lift it off); then move over 1 thread in fabric and punch needle through again. Continue this procedure, following pattern outline and using new strands of wine floss as needed. To end off a partially unused length of floss, clip off the

We've applied this beautiful technique to the Mid-Eastern caftan pattern given on page 11. A flock of graceful cranes swirls up around the neckline of the dress and across one sleeve. Variegated cotton embroidery floss gives the birds rich colorations.

You'll need: Igolochkoy needle (fig. 32-A); adjustable embroidery hoop 6 to 10″ in diameter; small scissors; pencil; yellow transfer pencil; 6-strand cotton embroidery floss in the following amounts and colors: 2 skeins wine, 6 skeins variegated cream-gold-rust (or equivalent), and 1 skein gold; Mid-Eastern caftan pattern pieces cut from preshrunk purple cotton.

piece out on flat surface, *wrong* side up; then cut tracings apart and arrange all birds but *one* #1 and *one* #2 around neck opening (fig. 32-B). When design is satisfactory, hold each tracing in place and transfer according to pencil directions. Position remaining 2 cranes on *wrong* side of left sleeve fabric pattern piece centered just above cuff fold; transfer.
3. Clip off 1-yard length of wine embroidery floss and separate 1 strand from 6-strand length. Moisten 1 end of strand and, holding needle point-down, drop moistened end of thread into funnel-shaped part of needle until

thread close to the *wrong* side of the fabric. Punchwork will look like a dotted line; turn fabric over to see loops.
5. When outline is completed, fill in neck and head area of bird with gold floss, moving back and forth in long, adjacent rows. Clip off excess thread.
6. Fill in center back area with wine-colored floss, working as in step 5.
7. Fill in bodies of birds with single strands of variegated floss, working out from body centers.
8. Repeat steps 4 through 7 for each remaining crane; then complete construction of caftan (see page 11). To set punchworked designs, machine wash garment in warm water.

Surface Decoration

Lovely products of an age-old Russian decorative technique, our igolochkoy cranes are worked with embroidery floss and a special hollow punch needle into a raised, plush design. Directions begin on page 32. Our Mid-Eastern Caftan (see page 11) forms the backdrop for these elegant decorations. Igolochkoy design: Jean Cook.

Ideas:

A. Igolochkoy in a modern vein—Peruvian art forms humorously reproduced as a "necklace" applied to a handmade smock. Design: Jean Cook. **B.** Symbolic flames and roses surround a central mandala, all hand-embroidered and set into a striking velvet evening dress. Design: Phyllis Mufson.

A

B

Surface Decoration

Sampler workshirt (upper right) is a good way to learn your embroidery stitches and end up with a wearable work of art in the bargain. Directions are on page 35. Design: Karen Cummings. Art nouveau floral embroidery (lower right) adorns a replica of our Mid-Eastern shirt with a reversed neck facing (see pages 8 and 11). Directions for this shirt are on page 36. Design: Carla Reed.

Ideas:

A. Rocky Mountain high-flying eagle spreads his beautiful hand-embroidered wings across a meticulously appliquéd and embroidered landscape. Design: Marinda Brown.

B. Richly colored western wildflowers have been hand-embroidered across this fringed, black satin shawl of an early 1920s pattern. Design: Andrea Shedletsky.

A

B

Sampler Workshirt

COLOR PHOTO ON PAGE 34

Learning embroidery stitches is a lot more fun when you can show an attractive finished embroidery for your efforts; and a decorative work shirt "sampler" really fills the bill. Work shirt fabric (usually a cotton blend) is easy to sew on, and it is easy to remove embroidery from a work shirt when you want to take out mistakes. Ten different stitches have been combined into a simple, interesting, overall yoke and cuff design.

You'll need: 1 ball perle cotton embroidery thread in *each* of the following colors: pale blue, sky blue, deep blue, indigo, lavender, grape, deep purple, leaf green, medium green, deep green, orange, apricot, and gold; small tapestry needle; scissors; pencil; small ruler; work shirt.

1. Mark a ½″-wide band at exact center of shirt yoke back, continuing band on collar up to collar fold. Measure 1 5/16″ to left of first band and draw in a similar ½″-wide band to collar fold. Repeat at right of center band. Measure another 1 5/16″ beyond each outside band and draw in a ½″-wide band on yoke only at either side to make 5 bands in all.

2. Embroider these bands in satin stitch (see page 26) using grape for center band, lavender for bands on right and left of center band, and deep purple for 2 outside bands. To match stitches and colors on either side, always work outward from center band.

3. Between center band and each lavender band embroider the following: 1 row indigo stem stitch (see page 26), 1 row sky blue chain stitch (see page 26), 1 row pale blue stem stitch, 1 row deep green leaves in lazy daisy stitch (fig. 35-A), 1 row orange flowers in lazy daisy stitch, 1 row deep green leaves in lazy daisy stitch, 1 row sky blue stem stitch, 1 row indigo chain stitch, 1 row medium green stem stitch.

4. Next, embroider areas between lavender and deep purple bands in this order: 1 row medium green stem stitch, 1 row indigo chain stitch, 1 row sky blue stem stitch, 1 row leaf green herringbone stitch (fig. 35-B), 1 row gold running stitch (fig. 35-C), 1 row leaf green herringbone stitch, 1 row sky blue stem stitch, 1 row deep blue chain stitch, 1 row apricot stem stitch.

5. Embroider last sampler areas on yoke beginning outside deep purple bands as follows: 1 row apricot stem stitch, 1 row deep blue chain stitch, 1 row sky blue stem stitch, 1 row deep

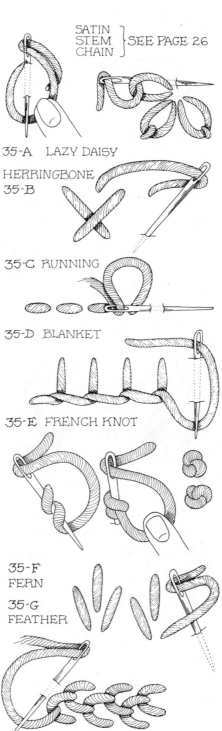

SATIN STEM CHAIN } SEE PAGE 26

35-A   LAZY DAISY

HERRINGBONE 35-B

35-C   RUNNING

35-D   BLANKET

35-E   FRENCH KNOT

35-F FERN

35-G FEATHER

green blanket stitch with 2 lows and 1 high (fig. 35-D). The last decorative stitch used on yoke is the French knot (fig. 35-E) in pale blue singles and gold triplets. Place French knots so that deep green blanket stitch highs meet gold triplets, and lows meet pale blue singles to form an overall floral motif.

6. To mark shirt cuffs, start at a point 3/16″ away from buttonhole and measure outward. Draw in four ½″-wide bands, each 1¼″ apart, across cuff. Repeat for remaining cuff.

7. To embroider cuffs, first fill in bands with satin stitch from buttonhole outward in this color order: lavender, deep purple, grape, lavender.

8. For areas between bands, work from buttonhole outward starting at left of first lavender band in this order: 1 row sky blue stem stitch, 1 row indigo chain stitch, 1 row medium green stem stitch.

9. Embroider the following between lavender and deep purple bands: 1 row deep green stem stitch, 1 row indigo chain stitch, 1 row sky blue stem stitch, 1 row deep green leaves in lazy daisy stitch, 1 row orange flowers in lazy daisy stitch, 1 row deep green leaves in lazy daisy stitch, 1 row pale blue stem stitch, 1 row sky blue chain stitch, 1 row indigo stem stitch.

10. Continue embroidery between deep purple and grape bands in this order: 1 row indigo stem stitch, 1 row sky blue chain stitch, 1 row pale blue stem stitch, 2 rows leaf green fern stitch (fig. 35-F) running down on the left and up on the right, 1 row sky blue stem stitch, 1 row deep blue chain stitch, 1 row apricot stem stitch.

11. Next, embroider between grape and 2nd lavender bands as follows: 1 row apricot stem stitch, 1 row deep blue chain stitch, 1 row sky blue stem stitch, 1 row medium green feather stitch (fig. 35-G) centered in open area with 2 rows orange lazy daisy stitches forming flowers at ends of feather stitches, 1 row deep green stem stitch, 1 row leaf green chain stitch, 1 row sky blue stem stitch.

12. Complete embroidery outside of last lavender band with: 1 row sky blue stem stitch, 1 row leaf green chain stitch, 1 row deep green stem stitch, 1 row deep green blanket stitch with 1 high and 2 lows. End with French knots in pale blue singles and gold triplets as in step 5.

Art Nouveau Floral Shirt

COLOR PHOTO ON PAGE 34

Fanciful coral-tone trumpet flowers and vines embroidered against a slubbed, off-white background make a lovely Art Nouveau-style frame for your face, especially when surrounded with the soft coral of our Mid-Eastern shirt (see page 11).

Only four embroidery stitches (see below)—stem, satin, long and short, and French knots—are used for the design, which is worked on a reversed neck facing (see page 8) cut in the shape of a large oval and fastened down with a double application of machine zigzag along the outer edge. The design is also applied to half-circle appliqués for each cuff.

The neck opening oval measures 6½ inches down from the shoulder line in front, 1½ inches down from shoulder line in back, and 6 inches wide at shoulder line. The depth of the facing at front is 6½ inches; from the back of the neck it measures 5 inches. The oval facing is 8¼ inches wide along the sides.

This facing is sized for a small woman's shirt; measurements will vary upward for larger sizes. To enlarge the embroidery design correspondingly, extend the length of all stems but keep the flowers and leaves in position. Add new leaves or buds to fill in any open spaces.

You'll need: 1 skein cotton embroidery floss in *each* of the following colors: buff (1), flesh (2), pale pink (3), light coral (4), medium coral (5), dark coral (6), red (7), yellow (8), pale green (9), light green (10), medium green (11), and dark green (12); embroidery hoop; embroidery needle; tissue paper; transfer pencil; scissors; off-white sewing thread; zigzag sewing machine; 1 yard slubbed, off-white cotton fabric (for facing); Mid-Eastern shirt pattern pieces in coral.

1. On scrap fabric, work out correct oval neck opening size to be used for shirt (see page 7).

2. Trace this neck opening onto tissue paper and construct facing around drawn neck opening, making slight size adjustments as needed. Use measurements given in introduction as guidelines for constructing facing shape.

3. Enlarge neckline floral design from graph (see page 24) and trace it onto tissue of oval facing. Do the same for cuff design. On *wrong* side of tissue, trace over embroidery designs and *outside* outlines of facing and cuff *only* with transfer pencil. Transfer 1 facing design to uncut off-white fabric, according to package directions; then transfer cuff design 4 times to uncut fabric (twice for each cuff). On neck facing design, add ⅝" to inner outline for seam allowance.

4. Using embroidery hoop, start with embroidery on cuff design. Follow color key at left, doing buds and stems first and ending with base of flower. Use stem stitch for stems; satin stitch for buds and flower bases.

5. Next, embroider designs which appear at back of shirt neckline (small bud with abbreviated stems). Work buds, bud base, and stems; then end with two-tone leaves and bud base.

6. Embroider front facing design last. Start with stems; then embroider leaves and buds. Follow with bud bases. Embroider trumpet flowers, starting at base and working up and outward to blossoms. Do stamens last, ending with French knots at each stamen tip. Also embroider 4 French knots at oval base of flower stalks.

7. Cut out and apply embroidered facing to shirt following directions on page 7 for applying reversed facing to shirt. Bind off raw edges of facing with 2 applications of machine zigzag using off-white thread.

8. Finish shirt up to step 4 of shirt directions on page 11. Before sewing side seams, apply sleeve decorations; bottoms of embroidered half-circles should fall ⅞" up from raw cuff edges. Pin into place and sew over all edges with 2 applications of machine zigzag using off-white thread.

9. Complete shirt according to directions given on page 11.

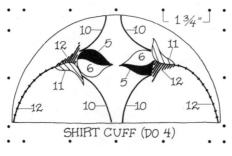

BACK

STITCHES

LONG AND SHORT: FLOWERS

STEM: SEPALS AND STEMS

SATIN: BUDS AND LEAVES

FRENCH KNOTS: DOTS

FRONT

SHIRT PANEL (DO 1)

OVERALL GRAPHIC PATTERNS SHOW COLOR AND FORM BREAKS

SHIRT CUFF (DO 4)

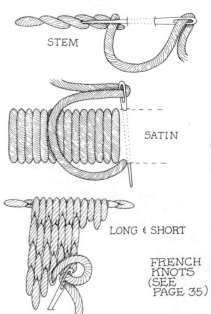

STEM

SATIN

LONG & SHORT

FRENCH KNOTS (SEE PAGE 35)

Poppycock T-shirt

COLOR PHOTO ON PAGE 39

Here's something any full-fledged nature lover will take to at first sight. This charming appliqué for a long-sleeved T-shirt can easily be made from scraps of fabric you may have on hand. Cut into simple shapes and bonded together layer by layer, the fabric pieces are outlined with machine zigzag stitching for graphic pizzaz.

You'll need: Large scraps of cotton (or equivalent) fabrics in the following colors and prints: yellow with floral print, periwinkle blue, light blue, red and blue check, white corduroy, red floral print, sky blue, orange and white polka dot, black paisley print, chartreuse, pale green, and green and white print; ¼ yard iron-on bonding; 1 spool medium brown cotton thread; tissue paper; pencil; scissors; zigzag sewing machine; iron; long-sleeved red T-shirt.

1. Enlarge pattern below to correct size on tissue paper (see page 24) and trace individual patterns for all parts of flower and for both circular backgrounds. Cut out tissue patterns; then cut patterns from appropriate fabrics (use color photo on page 39 as your guide), adding a ¼" seam allowance for all pattern edges which are overlapped by another edge or other parts of appliqué design.
2. Cut all pattern pieces from iron-on bonding to exact pattern size without seam allowance.
3. With iron set at temperature indicated by bonding manufacturer, bond the fabric pieces together layer by layer in this order; large yellow print circle, periwinkle blue circle, light blue scallop wedge, red and blue checked curved band across scallop, white stamens, red floral print petal row, sky blue petal row, orange polka dot outer petals, black paisley sepal, green and white print stem, pale green stem head, chartreuse half-leaf and pale green half-leaf (at left of stem), and chartreuse leaf. Use enlarged pattern as placement guide.
4. Set sewing machine stitch guides for 15 stitches per inch and ¼" in width. Sew at low speed to allow for hand manipulation of fabric.
5. With brown thread, zigzag over all raw fabric edges except for outside raw edge of entire appliqué.
6. Bond entire appliqué to T-shirt and zigzag over the raw outer edge of finished appliqué.

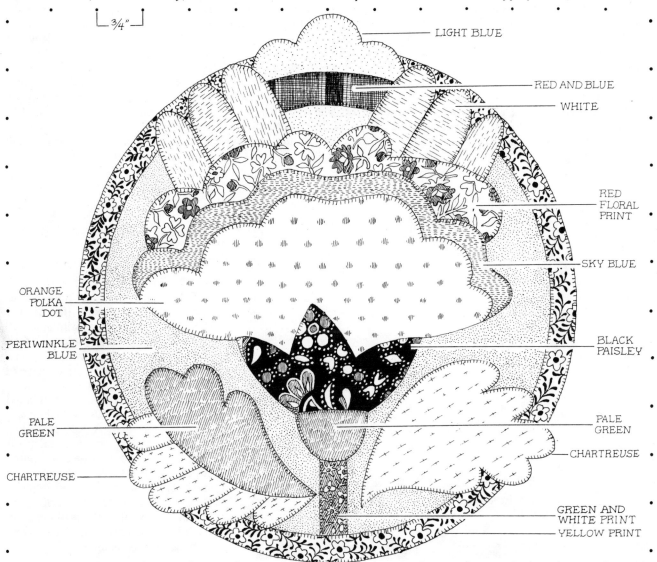

3/4"

LIGHT BLUE

RED AND BLUE

WHITE

RED FLORAL PRINT

SKY BLUE

BLACK PAISLEY

PALE GREEN

CHARTREUSE

GREEN AND WHITE PRINT

YELLOW PRINT

ORANGE POLKA DOT

PERIWINKLE BLUE

PALE GREEN

CHARTREUSE

Piece-patched Shirt

COLOR PHOTO ON PAGE 39

It is easy to add excitement to a basic shape such as the Mid-Eastern shirt pattern used here (described in detail on page 11); just patchwork each pattern piece from simple color groupings of related fabrics before sewing the garment together.

We've used color-related swatches of small print cottons in blues, browns, and cream with a panel of Japanese ikat-dyed fabric to tie the look together. Accented here and there with touches of purple and green, the shirt includes a simple yet striking combination of colors.

To mix up a batch of patches, select materials from your own collection of yardage scraps or purchase fabric in related colors. Collect fabrics of similar weight and appearance (lightweight cottons work best) and arrange them to focus attention on one or two areas of the shirt. We've chosen bands of pieced strips located on both

sleeves and on both sides of the center panel as focal points.

Note: We have given yardage amounts for a medium-size shirt; before purchasing fabric, see "Your Pattern Key," page 9.

You'll need: 2 yards of Japanese ikat-dyed fabric (or equivalent); 2 yards of blue with white floral print fabric; ¼ yard lightweight purple cotton fabric; ½ yard white with blue floral print fabric; thirty-five 3½ by 4" rectangles of cotton fabric in various shades of blue, brown, ochre, magenta, green, and cream (or equivalent); 2 spools black thread; 1 package black wide bias seam tape; paper pattern for Mid-Eastern shirt; ruler; pencil; scissors; iron; tailor's chalk.

1. Divide pattern pieces into proportional divisions (fig. 38-A). No specific measurements are given for dividing each pattern piece as these will vary with size of shirt to be made. Mark each division as in figure 38-A. Cut each pattern apart on division lines.
2. Cut *each* division of *each* pattern piece (except for all pieced strips) from appropriate fabrics, first adding ⅝" seam allowance to all *division* edges. (Add no seam allowances if ikat fabric is used; it is originally woven 14" wide—more than enough room to include both seams.)

3. To make pieced strips for both sleeves, select eighteen 3½ by 4" rectangles and divide into 3 groups of 6 rectangles each. Arrange colors in a pleasing sequence in each group; then sew all 4" sides together with ¼" seams to make three 6-rectangle strips. Press seams flat. Cut strips in half lengthwise (fig. 38-B). Separate each pair of identical strips to form 2 matching groups containing 3 strips each. Select 2 strips from 1 group and join them along 1 long edge, using a ¼" seam allowance as in fig. 38-C. Repeat for same 2 strips from 2nd group. Iron under raw edges of *all* strips.
4. Sew sleeve pieces A, B, and C together for both sleeves; then topstitch 1/16" away from either side of each seam to hold seam allowances.
5. Measure ½" down from B/C seam on each sleeve and pin remaining single strips from step 3 to each sleeve at these points. Measure 8½" up from cuff edges and pin a double strip from step 3 to each sleeve at these points. Topstitch all strips into place.
6. For long fabric strips (E) on center panel of shirt (D), join seventeen 3½ by 4" cotton print rectangles end to end in *one* long strip as in step 3. Press seams flat; then cut strip in half *lengthwise* to make two strips.

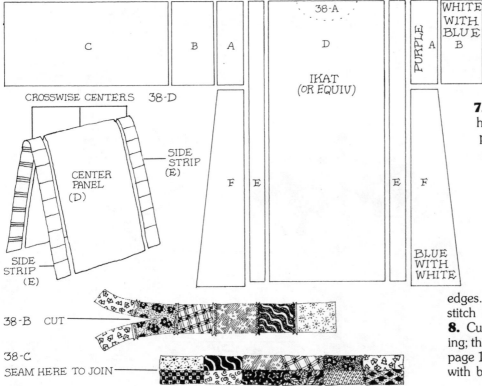

7. Fold strips and center panel in half crosswise to find center points and mark (fig. 38-D). Iron under approximately ¼" along *one* long edge of each pieced strip. Lay center panel flat; then lay folded edge of each strip over each long edge of panel (combined width should equal measurement A—see page 11). Match center marks on strips to those on panel edges. Pin strips into place and topstitch 1/16" in from folded edge.
8. Cut and sew desired neck opening; then construct shirt as directed on page 11. Finish hem and sleeve edges with black bias seam tape.

Surface Decoration

Piece-Patched Shirt (left) and Poppycock T-shirt (right) projects are worked in patchwork and machine appliqué, respectively. Patterns begin on page 37 for the T-shirt and on page 38 for the pieced shirt (also see page 11). T-shirt design: Nancy Freeman. Pieced shirt design: Alyson Gonsalves and Patricia Scarlett.

Ideas:

A. Intricately pieced squares cut from 1940s fabrics patchwork into a coat of humorous distinction. Design: Stacy Sussman.

B. Traditional Guatemalan Indian designs are the inspiration for this machine appliquéd and embroidered corduroy dress. Design: Karen Baxter-Foster.

A

B

Ideas for Surface Decoration

A *tour de force* of fantastic ideas for surface decoration, these uniquely beautiful garments are the handwork of advanced or professional clothing decorators. We've included them as suggestions for ways in which you can put materials, colors, and shapes to new, exciting uses on your own decorated clothing. For more advanced and professional ideas, turn to pages 16, 17, 56, 57, and 79.

A. Machine knitted elements join with the solid body of this multicolored sweater to make angular edgings on hem and on cuffs. Design: Marika Contompasis.

B, C. Fanciful feathered halter top of peacock, pheasant, and rooster feathers is hand-knotted to a macraméd deerskin thong base. Design: Raoul Speigel. Sky, sea, and land come together in

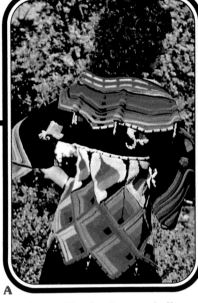

A

the form of bird pelts, seashells, and graceful leather tassels collaged onto a leather cape. Design: Nicki Marx.

D, E. One-of-a-kind jacket pieced from hand-woven fabric features intricately worked, padded tapestry back panel and fringed cuffs.
Design: Valerie Dearing. An air of simple dignity surrounds "Cloak for Endymion," a hand-woven garment with tapestry and space-wrapped fleece decorations. Design: Barbara Setsu Pickett.

F, G. Ribbons, rickrack, trims, and Seminole patchwork harmonize with handmade tassels and a painted

B

C

D

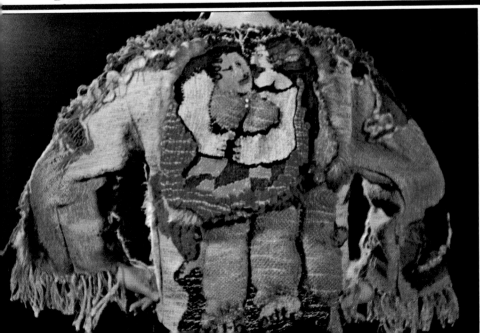

E

mandala to produce a dress of distinction. Design: Linda Witt.
Simple yet elegant pieced and tucked garment, a style similar to our Mid-Eastern caftan pattern, puts Seminole patchwork to good use. Design: Hope Hightower.

H. Antique laces, trims, and embroidery are artfully pieced to create this elaborately trimmed blouson. Design: Jessica Overstreet.

I. Unusual pieced and quilted jacket with winged epaulets and cuffs

makes clever use of stripes and colors. Design: Cuca.

J. "Sunshine's Rainbow Cape" creates a fantasy world of carefully cut and machine appliquéd fabrics. Design: Colette.

F
I

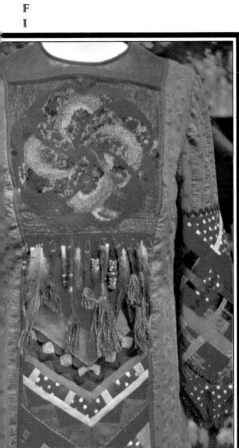

G

H

J

Dyes and Paints

Two beauties: Our handpainted, pieced chamois shirt with lacings (below, left) and a clamp-and-dye silk poncho (below, right). Each has a distinctive appearance sure to draw appreciative looks and compliments. Directions for the chamois shirt are on page 44. Design: K. Lee Manuel. Directions for the clamp-and-dye poncho are on page 45. Design: Alyson Gonsalves. Concept: Marian Clayden.

Ideas:

A. Especially applied to fit the dress pattern pieces, deep shades of purple and green tie-dye are spiced with accents of yellow. Design: Lois Ziff Brooks.
B. Handpainted designs based on dream images produced "Tibetan Dream Dress," a fantasy garment trimmed with hand-dyed ribbon fringe. Design: K. Lee Manuel.

A

B

Dyes & Paints

Dyes and paints are an exciting and relatively easy way to quickly create impressive visual effects in clothing. The following information is intended as a general introduction to the use of dyes and paints. For more specific material, consult the instruction sheets that accompany each type of dye or paint. Some dye and paint sources are listed on page 78.

DOING IT WITH DYES

There are many types of dyes. With some you use hot dyebaths (best for tie-dyeing and piece-dyeing, as heat produces brilliance and better color fastness); others are applied at room temperature (best for batiks, whose wax will melt at high temperatures). For our projects we've selected two of the most commonly available and most widely used dyes—fiber reactive dyes and household dyes.

Fiber reactive dyes. For use with all natural fibers, and formulated to be used in a room-temperature dyebath, fiber reactive dyes produce colors that are strong and very colorfast. These dyes, found at craft and yarn supply stores, create an actual chemical bond between the dye and the cloth fibers. They are packaged under a number of names, and the only difference between the brands offered is the inclusion or noninclusion of salt and washing soda assistants with the dye. Note: Since the washing soda is caustic, it can eat away wax from batiks. Be sure to check your batik between dyebaths and rewax if necessary.

Household dyes. These commonly available dyes are found most often in grocery and dime stores. Because they consist of a blend of dye types, they can color synthetics and blends, as well as natural fibers. Used as a hot dyebath, they initially produce bright colors, but repeated machine washing will dull their colors quickly. Either hand-wash or dry-clean household-dyed fabrics. Household dyes also use salt (or vinegar, if wool is being dyed) as a catalyst.

Equipment. Dyeing equipment can be purchased at a good hardware or dime store. The list would include an enamel or stainless steel pan (or a plastic bucket in the case of cold-water dyes) to hold the dyebath (do not use an aluminum container, as it would discolor your dyebath), a plastic or glass measuring cup and spoons, a wooden dowel or large plastic spoon for stirring, and good rubber gloves. Plan to wear an old apron or old clothes—dye is hard to remove once you've been splashed.

Each dye packet will give specifics about the amounts of dye and catalyst required for a given amount of fabric. Also remember that you can't judge dye color intensity by the appearance of the dyebath itself.

To avoid allergic reactions or respiratory and skin irritations, handle dyes carefully. Don't allow dye powder to get into the air; wear rubber gloves at all times while handling dyes; don't eat or smoke while dyeing; work only in the bathroom or laundry, not in the kitchen; and clean up thoroughly until all dye color is absent from your work area.

Here are general steps to follow:

1. Measure correct amount of dye powder into cup. Note: At this stage basic dye colors can be mixed to create new colors.

2. Add a small amount of hot water to dye and mix into a lumpless paste.

3. Fill dyebath container with just enough water at correct temperature to cover fabric.

4. Add dye paste to dyebath.

5. Mix in dye catalyst.

6. Completely wet fabric in clear water and wring out excess; then immerse in dyebath.

7. Frequently stir fabric around in dyebath for even dyeing. For batiks, cup-baste instead to avoid excess cracking of wax. Note: At this stage fiber reactive dyes require the addition of 2 to 3 tablespoons of dissolved washing soda to fix the dye color.

8. When fabric is three shades darker than desired, remove it from dyebath and rinse thoroughly in running water.

9. Wash in warm, soapy water, rinse, and blot away excess water. For batiks and piece-dyed fabric, lay out flat and allow to air-dry out of direct sun. Dry tie-dyed cloth completely before removing ties.

10. To set colors, steam iron piece-dyed or tie-dyed cloth for 5 to 10 minutes. Sandwich batiks between layers of *old* newsprint and iron with a dry iron until most of the wax has been soaked up by the paper.

11. Be sure to clean working area thoroughly. An abrasive bleach cleanser will remove dye stains from work area. To remove dye from skin, apply a mild solution of liquid bleach and warm water, then rinse skin thoroughly and apply hand lotion.

12. Dyebaths should be disposed of. Store dye powders and dye pastes in a dark, cool place in clearly labeled glass containers.

THE PLEASURES OF TEXTILE PAINTS

Unlike dyes, textile paints can be used with a minimum of detailed instructions; in fact, they are used in much the same way as regular paints.

Three types of paint can be used on fabrics: acrylic, a water-base plastic paint that coats the surface of fabric, leaving a slightly stiff surface when air-dried; true textile paint, which is formulated to penetrate the fabric and coat individual fibers, and which is set by ironing; and vat dye, a pigment similar to fiber reactive dyes that produces a chemical bond with fabric when activated by heat or light.

Acrylics and textile paints can be mixed and used like regular paints; vat dyes, which are colorless in their original state, are difficult to judge during mixing. Equipment and brushes used with these paints are easily cleaned with soapy water.

Note: for information on enlarging and transferring designs see page 24.

Indian-style Chamois Shirt

COLOR PHOTO ON PAGE 42

A "noble savage"—our hand-painted chamois shirt trimmed with lacing and beads. Open lacing along the sides makes the fit adjustable.

Chamois can be treated just like a fine woolen when it needs a cleaning—but you *must* avoid steam or moisture during the drying process; it will shrink or stiffen the leather. Hand wash this shirt in cold water with a mild soap, gently squeezing the water through the garment (never scrub or pull); then lay the shirt out flat and allow to dry *completely*. To soften the leather, toss the *dry* garment into a *dry* dryer; iron wrinkles with *dry* iron.

You'll need: Two 24 by 30″ and two 7 by 17″ pieces of buff chamois; 44 yards of ⅛″-wide buff chamois or buckskin lacing; 1 jar textile paint in *each* of the following colors: red, yellow, blue, violet, black, and white (all colors used on the shirt are mixed from these basic colors); 1 quart isopropyl alcohol; several stiff-bristle brushes; plate or paint palette; clothes dryer or iron; 100 black coconut palm hishi beads and 16 red stone hishi beads; #0 leather hole hinge-punch; hammer; scissors; pencil; pattern paper; ruler; 2 by 4″ soft pine wood.

1. Enlarge half-patterns and designs; transfer to folded pattern paper (see page 24). Cut out and unfold.
2. Lay 1 piece of chamois out on flat surface and tape down. Align front panel pattern on leather so that bottom edge coincides with uneven edge of chamois. Front and back side seams can be cut to match or left uneven for a more natural look. Tape pattern down; cut out front panel.
3. Using a blunt pencil, trace over punch hole placements and outline design areas on garment pattern. This will leave indentations and grooves in leather beneath. Remove pattern, and pencil lines lightly onto chamois.

4. Repeat steps 2 and 3 for back panel and sleeves.
5. Punch out all holes with #0 punch; use pine as a cutting surface.
6. Mix your colors from paints you've purchased (see below); then add enough isopropyl alcohol as an extender to make paints flow onto leather—alcohol gives paint more permanency. Using bristle brushes and following color indicators on pattern, paint in design areas one color at a time, working from light to dark.
7. Allow paints to dry completely. Set colors using dry dryer or dry iron.
8. Cut lacing into following amounts and sizes: fifty 12″ lengths, thirty-two 16″ lengths, and sixteen 24″ lengths; then taper both ends of each length.
9. Lace shoulders together, using one 12″ lace for *every* 2 holes. Lap front shoulder edge over back and lace down through both layers of first hole, and then up through both layers of second hole; center lacing and tie knots at base of *each* end to secure.
10. Attach sleeves to shoulders using 16″ lengths of lacing by overlapping sleeve holes over shoulder holes and lacing through as in step 9. Do not knot. Instead, string a coconut shell hishi onto each lacing end and push it down to rest on seam.
11. Attach 12″ laces along painted design on front of shirt as in step 9 and knot each at its base. Knot a coconut shell hishi at end of each lace.
12. Knot remaining 12″ laces into holes running along painted design on back panel of shirt.
13. Knot a 24″ length of lacing into each pair of holes along shirt sides and thread a red stone hishi over each pair of ends, pushing it up lacings to surface of chamois. Use these laces to close up sides of shirt.

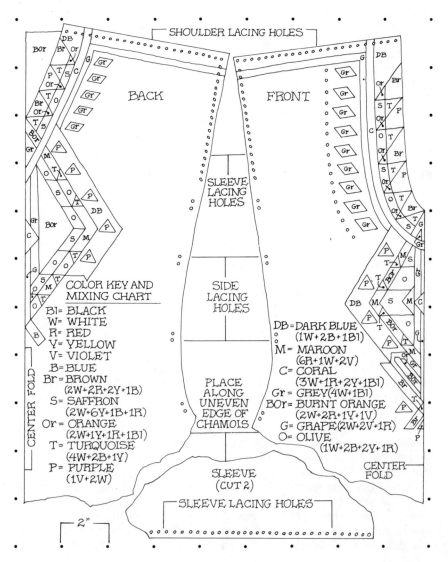

COLOR KEY AND MIXING CHART

Bl = BLACK
W = WHITE
R = RED
Y = YELLOW
V = VIOLET
B = BLUE
Br = BROWN (2W+2R+2Y+1B)
S = SAFFRON (2W+6Y+1B+1R)
Or = ORANGE (2W+1Y+1R+1Bl)
T = TURQUOISE (4W+2B+1Y)
P = PURPLE (1V+2W)

DB = DARK BLUE (1W+2B+1Bl)
M = MAROON (6R+1W+2V)
C = CORAL (3W+1R+2Y+1Bl)
Gr = GREY (4W+1Bl)
BOr = BURNT ORANGE (2W+2R+1V+1V)
G = GRAPE (2W+2V+1R)
O = OLIVE (1W+2B+2Y+1R)

Clamp and Dye Poncho

COLOR PHOTO ON PAGE 42

Motifs cut from plywood or plastic sheeting join forces with a simple bleaching process to produce a really gorgeous silk top. Though only three dye colors are used, many more shades and colors emerge, thanks to dye overlaps, held-back areas, and the final discharge process.

You'll need: 1¼ yards 42"-wide white China silk cut into a 42 by 42" square; 1 packet all-purpose household dye in *each* of the following colors: plum, peacock, and canary yellow; 1 packet dye color remover; uniodized salt; two 1 sq. ft. pieces of plywood or clear plastic; jigsaw or coping saw; 4 small C-clamps; large stainless steel or enameled bowl or roasting pan; rubber gloves; stirring rods; glass measuring cup; plastic squeeze bottle; 1 spool *each* yellow and blue sewing thread; fine needle.

1. The day before: preshrink silk. Also, copy freehand shapes shown below onto one of plywood or plastic sheets. Clamp second sheet of plywood or plastic under first; then use coping or jigsaw to cut out 2 identical shapes for each motif. Cut scraps into 8 rectangles, each slightly larger than cut-out shapes.

2. Dye process: Wearing rubber gloves at all times, mix 1 teaspoon plum dye in glass cup with enough water to make smooth paste. Add required salt and enough water to give mixture a thin, watery consistency. Pour dye into squeeze bottle and set aside.

3. Prepare canary yellow dyebath in bowl or pan following package directions.

4. To prepare silk for dyeing, thoroughly wet and fold it into quarters; then, at upper right corner (where center of fabric is folded), carefully squirt down a 2 by 7" diagonal line of plum dye; be sure to penetrate all 4 layers of silk (fig. 45-A). Sandwich *all 4 layers* of plum-color silk between matching wave shapes, aligning wave edges exactly. Position plywood or clear plastic scrap over top and bottom waves; then clamp "sandwich" tight with small C-clamp.

5. Gather folded silk diagonally (fig. 45-B) and dip half of silk with clamped motifs into yellow dye bath. Simmer submerged portion until 3 shades darker than desired color. Re-move silk from dyebath and rinse in cool water until rinse runs clear. Leave clamped motif attached.

6. Lay quartered silk out flat with dyed portion pointing toward upper left. About 6" up from lower right corner, sandwich all 4 layers of silk between heart-shaped motifs. Clamp.

7. Discard yellow dyebath and rinse out container. Make up peacock dyebath in clean container according to package instructions. Gather up silk diagonally, but grasp slightly *above* bottom of yellow-dyed area; submerge remaining silk in dyebath. Allow blue dye to creep into yellow-dyed area to form green. Rinse.

8. Pour out blue dyebath and rinse out container. Mix color remover in clean container according to package directions.

9. Lay folded silk out as in step 6; then prepare it for color removal by unclamping heart motifs, folding up lower right edge and corner, and repositioning and reclamping heart motifs over white heart-shaped areas and additional 4 layers of blue silk. Also make a fold 5" in from lower left edge of silk and clamp long rectangle motif, as in step 4, at edge and close to fold (fig. 45-C).

Next, fold quartered, clamped silk into a triangle, matching up lower left and upper right corners. Using yellow corner of scarf as your pivot point, fold silk into a long cone shape and clamp last motif lengthwise within green area (fig. 45-D).

10. Holding silk by yellow end, submerge silk into color remover up to green area. Constantly move area where silk enters dyebath to prevent a strong line from forming. Watch this process carefully—color remover works quickly. When blue area has turned light turquoise, remove silk and rinse *thoroughly*. Unclamp all motifs and set aside. Rinse silk again; then allow to air-dry out of direct sun.

11. To make top, fold silk diagonally into a 2-layered triangle. Find center of folded edge and place 2 marks along edge, each 6½" out from center point. Open out silk, lightly join marks with pencil line and carefully cut from mark to mark along this line. Using yellow thread and a fine needle, handroll neck opening (fig. 45-E). Handroll all edges of top with blue thread to complete.

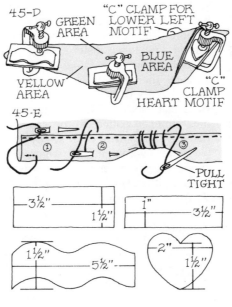

45-A PLUM DYE THROUGH ALL FOUR LAYERS — SILK FOLDED INTO QUARTERS

45-B PLASTIC WAVE MOTIF SCRAP — "C" CLAMP — RUBBER GLOVES

45-C MOTIF — SCRAP — "C" CLAMP MOTIF — "C" CLAMP — SCRAP "C" CLAMP

45-D GREEN AREA — "C" CLAMP FOR LOWER LEFT MOTIF — BLUE AREA — YELLOW AREA — "C" CLAMP HEART MOTIF

45-E PULL TIGHT — 3½" — 1½" — 1" — 3½" — 1½" — 5½" — 2" — 1½"

Bold Batik Dress

COLOR PHOTO ON PAGE 47

For sheer visual impact you can't go wrong with this combination of a bold, batiked design and the simple, flowing lines of our Oriental dress pattern (see page 13). Successive applications of melted wax resist alternate with light and dark dyebaths to produce a subtle graphic design in teal blue and deep purple on a mottled white background.

Because of its size, this project must be dyed in a bathtub to avoid excessive cracking of the wax resist.

You'll need: Fiber reactive dyes in the following colors: lemon yellow, scarlet, navy blue, and black; uniodized salt and washing soda (if specified in package instructions); 2 lb. half paraffin/half beeswax batik wax; plastic gloves; 1 gallon cleaning fluid (optional—instead, the garment may be taken to a good dry cleaner for wax removal); 1 small, 1 medium, and 1 large inexpensive soft-bristle brushes; candy thermometer; one 1-lb. coffee can and 1 asbestos hot pad or double boiler; an electric hot plate or electric stove (*Note: Do not* use gas burners to melt wax); baking soda (to douse any accidentally ignited wax—*do not* use water to put out a wax fire); a plastic dropcloth; Oriental Dress pattern (with neck opening drawn but *not* cut out) cut from prewashed 40''-wide silk—extra silk must be sewn to each sleeve to make it wrist-length; blue dressmaker's carbon; tracing wheel; 1 large spool white silk or mercerized cotton thread; pins; scissors; pencil; ruler.

1. Fold dress in half at shoulder and align side seams; pin; then lay folded dress out, front *up*, on a hard, flat surface. Fold dress in half again down center front so that only one-quarter of dress shows. This will simplify application of design and allow you to line up and mark design areas at seams and elsewhere to ensure design match-ups.

2. Following design layout in figure 46-A, transfer design freehand to dress with pencil (no specific enlargements are given for design—this will vary with size of garment being made).

3. When design is applied to one-quarter of dress, open front out flat; complete design by connecting marks made at seams.

4. To transfer design to back of dress, lay dressmaker's carbon out on flat

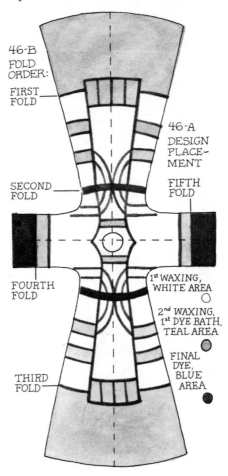

46-B
FOLD
ORDER:

FIRST
FOLD

SECOND
FOLD

FOURTH
FOLD

THIRD
FOLD

46-A
DESIGN
PLACE-
MENT

FIFTH
FOLD

1st WAXING,
WHITE AREA

2nd WAXING,
1st DYE BATH,
TEAL AREA

FINAL
DYE,
BLUE
AREA

surface, carbon up; then fold dress in half at shoulders and lay out over carbon. Trace over front design with tracing wheel to transfer design.

5. Spread out dropcloth on large, flat surface; then lay unfolded and unpinned dress out on plastic.

6. Break wax into large chunks and melt either in coffee can on asbestos pad-covered burner or in top of double boiler over simmering water. Use candy thermometer to monitor wax, keeping it between 350° and 400°F.

7. Apply first layer of wax with medium and large brushes to all areas that are to remain white. *No wax* should touch or cover any pencil lines or marks; these must be concealed by dye. During application, wax must look completely transparent for it to

have penetrated fabric completely. Recoat any areas where wax appears white, to impregnate all fibers thoroughly. Rewax any areas on reverse side of fabric where wax has not penetrated. Allow all wax to dry.

8. Your first dyebath will contain 1 part lemon yellow dye, 4 parts navy blue dye, and 1 part black dye. Divide *each* dye color into 6 equal piles; then mix together 1 pile of yellow, 4 piles of blue, and 1 pile of black to make up equivalent of 1 complete packet of dye. Set remaining dye powders aside.

9. Read thoroughly through instructions accompanying dyes; then prepare 1st dyebath accordingly. Fill bathtub with 6'' of water at 90° to 100°F; then add dye mixture and any other ingredients necessary. Mix dyebath thoroughly.

10. Fold waxed garment along areas containing no wax (in order to prevent unwanted cracks) until it is slightly smaller than bathtub (see fig. 46-B for order of folds). Wearing plastic gloves, immerse garment in dyebath; then gently circulate dye by hand during dyeing to promote complete dye penetration. Allow garment to steep until dyed areas become 3 shades darker than desired; then remove dress and rinse in cold water until water runs clear. Lay garment out flat on dropcloth; allow to dry completely.

11. Before next waxing, check over original waxing and repair chips or large cracks with fresh wax; then following step 7, apply melted wax to those areas which will remain teal, the color of 1st dyebath.

12. Your 2nd dyebath will contain 3 parts navy blue dye, 1 part black dye, and a generous pinch of scarlet dye. Combine these colors as described in step 8; add scarlet dye last.

13. Prepare 2nd dyebath as in step 9; then, folding garment as indicated in figure 46-B, repeat step 10.

14. Make a thick pad of newspapers and cover with paper toweling. To remove wax resist, saturate garment with cleaning fluid, one area at a time, and blot with more paper towels. Discard saturated towels in a well-ventilated place; replace with fresh towels.

15. When all wax is removed, complete construction of garment according to directions on page 13; then wash dress in detergent and warm water to remove cleaning fluid.

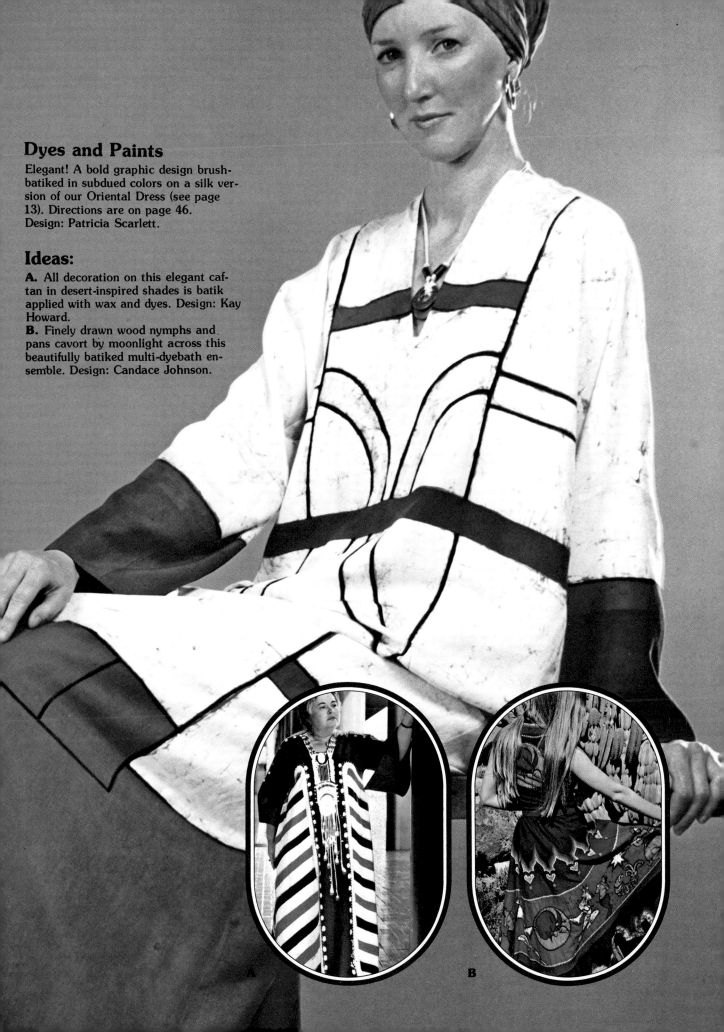

Dyes and Paints

Elegant! A bold graphic design brush-batiked in subdued colors on a silk version of our Oriental Dress (see page 13). Directions are on page 46. Design: Patricia Scarlett.

Ideas:

A. All decoration on this elegant caftan in desert-inspired shades is batik applied with wax and dyes. Design: Kay Howard.

B. Finely drawn wood nymphs and pans cavort by moonlight across this beautifully batiked multi-dyebath ensemble. Design: Candace Johnson.

Painted Iron-on Patches

COLOR PHOTO ON PAGE 49

Ever wonder if there's a more exciting way to fix a hole or a tear in clothing than by conventional darning and patching? Look no further. Here's the means to give not only a patch, but a pat on the back, to your favorite kid.

Commercially available iron-on patches can be transformed from plain to powerful with a few volts of bright color if you use textile paint. There are several types of textile paints available in tube form, each providing a clean, easy way for you or your child to decorate almost any kind of fabric. Your local hobby or dime store will probably carry these paints; if not, consult the supply list on page 78.

You'll need: 1 tube textile paint in *each* of the following colors: bright orange, dark orange, yellow, bright blue, dark blue, and red; four 5 by 6″ white iron-on patches; dressmaker's carbon; hard lead pencil; scissors; iron; jeans jacket.

1. Using dressmaker's carbon, transfer patterns at right onto white patches with pencil. Trace pattern lightly to avoid leaving dark lines.

2. Outline designs with paint in colors indicated on pattern. Hold tubes straight up and down, not on a slant, so the color flows properly from tube to patch (fig. 48-A). Work slowly and evenly, squeezing out more paint as needed to completely penetrate fabric. Don't worry if paint won't penetrate through glue backing of patch—it is not supposed to.

3. When outlines are completed, fill in solid areas of designs with appropriate colors. Again, work slowly and evenly for best results.

4. Carefully cut out finished designs and arrange on jacket to be decorated. Following manufacturer's directions, iron each patch in place.

5. Let patches set for 2 weeks before washing, to avoid bleeding colors.

ACTUAL SIZE CUT 2

ACTUAL SIZE CUT 1 OF ENTIRE LARGE PATCH CUT 5 OF SMALL STAR CIRCLE BELOW

FIG. 48-A

HOLD UPRIGHT

DO <u>NOT</u> SLANT

Dyes and Paints

Spice up our French Chef's Apron Pattern with vegetable prints (left). Directions are on page 50. Design: Nancy Papa. Painted iron-on patches (below) brighten a denim jacket. Directions are on page 48. Design: Karen Cummings.

Idea:
Eerie "Night Train" shirt, cut from pattern similar to that on page 13, was handpainted with vat dyes. Design: Ken McDonald.

Vegetable Printed Apron

COLOR PHOTO ON PAGE 49

Though chefs' aprons are traditionally an understated white, they make a perfect vehicle for surface decoration. One quick and easy way to add an individual touch to your cooking garb is to give vegetables commonly used in cooking a second function—as printing blocks.

You'll need: 1 *each* of the following vegetables: corn ear, celery stalk with leaves, carrot with leaves, small head of cabbage, and turnip; 1 jar textile paints in each of the following colors: orange, green, yellow, red, and brown; inexpensive woven placemat; inexpensive ¾"-wide paint brush; small tapered paint brush; paper towels; kitchen knife; scissors; old newspapers; masking tape; T-pins; pencil; iron; extra fabric scraps; French Chef's Apron and pocket (page 22).

1. Cut all vegetables (except celery and corn) in half lengthwise and place face down on paper towels to dry for several hours. Remove carrot top and, pressing celery and carrot leaves under heavy books to flatten, set aside.

2. Trace pattern below; then fold woven placemat in half. Using pattern as cutting guide, cut bowl shape from placemat (fig. 50-A); unfold.

3. Form a smooth, firm, but slightly springy printing surface from a stack of newspapers laid out and taped down with masking tape (fig. 50-B).

4. Pin pocket of apron to newspaper pad, keeping it as flat as possible.

5. Use ¾"-wide brush to apply brown fabric paint to surface of bowl shape. Center bowl over upper middle of pocket along top edge and press down hard on shape to print.

6. Coat carrot cross-section with orange fabric paint and make a test print on fabric scrap. If test print appears too heavy or too light, adjust application of paint accordingly. Recoat carrot and print below and to left of (slightly overlapping) bowl. Coat carrot leaves with green paint. Place leaves leading from carrot head across pocket bottom toward right edge. Print, using a paper towel to press carrot leaves into place.

7. Remove pocket; allow to dry.

8. Pin apron over newspaper pad, keeping it as flat as possible. Mark lightly with pencil where pocket will be sewn to apron.

9. Make another mark at center of apron slightly below top edge of pocket placement. Starting with carrots, print vegetables in appropriate colors from right to left in a fanlike arrangement. To print celery and corn ear, coat each with paint and roll slightly against fabric. Use paper towels to press down celery leaves. Print turnip last.

10. To add contrasting color on carrots, paint in ridges with small brush.

11. Remove apron from pad and allow to dry. Rinse out both brushes. To set paint when thoroughly dry, iron design for 5 minutes with hot iron.

12. Sew pocket to apron, positioning basket to "hold" printed vegetables.

50-A

FOLDED PLACEMAT

CUT AROUND PATTERN SHAPE

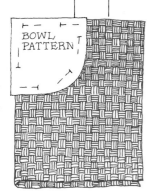

BOWL PATTERN

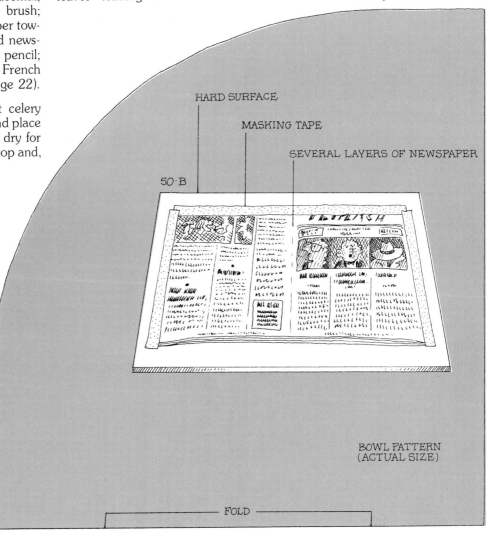

50·B

HARD SURFACE

MASKING TAPE

SEVERAL LAYERS OF NEWSPAPER

BOWL PATTERN (ACTUAL SIZE)

FOLD

Dyes and Paints

Floral-patterned skirt (below) and "color-me-in" pocket pinafore (right) are both decorated with silkscreen-printed designs. Textile paints are used to color the pinafore pocket, something your child may enjoy doing. Directions for both projects begin on page 52. Skirt design: Jayne and Gary Lomax. Pocket design: Vea Van Kessel.

Idea:

Strong, silkscreened design motifs of this hooded jacket conjure up thoughts of Matisse or early American "tulip" quilt appliqués. Design: Deborah Slabeck and Kathleen Ozorio.

Silk-screened Skirt and Pinafore

COLOR PHOTO ON PAGE 51

Silkscreening is an enjoyable way to make inexpensive multiples of a design. All supplies can be purchased at your local art supply center or ordered from the sources listed on page 78. Though a number of stencil techniques are possible, we've chosen two of the most interesting—cut-film stencil (the skirt) and photostencil (the pinafore pocket)—for you to try as decorative applications.

The silkscreen itself is actually a fine mesh fabric of silk, organdy, or polyester open-weave cloth secured to a frame, to which different kinds of printing stencils may be attached. A squeegee, or rubber-bladed wooden wedge, is pulled across the screen-mounted stencil to force ink down through the exposed mesh of the screen *not* blocked by the stencil and onto a printing surface positioned beneath the open screen area.

MAKE YOUR OWN SILKSCREEN

To make a silkscreen, join four 1 by 2″ lengths of unwarped pine securely at their ends to form a sturdy frame. The overall inside frame dimensions should equal the largest size design you plan to print plus a 2″ margin on sides and a 4″ margin on ends.

To this frame, tack and stretch a rectangle of screen fabric cut 1″ larger than the *outer* dimensions of the frame (fig. 52-A). Work from the center of each frame side out to the corners, tightly stretching the screen evenly from top to bottom, then side to side to prevent distortion of its weave pattern. Trim off excess screen fabric.

To seal screen edge to wood frame, cover entire inner side of frame with paper tape, lapping it over onto the screen. Paint over tape and along screen edge on both sides of screen

with orange shellac (fig. 52-B); allow to dry completely.

Cut a rectangle of ¼″-thick plywood 3″ larger all around than the outside dimensions of the frame. This piece will be used as a printing base. Attach the frame to the base with two removable pin hinges to allow the frame to be detached for stencil application, large-surface printing, and cleanup.

When cut, your squeegee should be 2″ shorter than the smallest inside dimension of your screen.

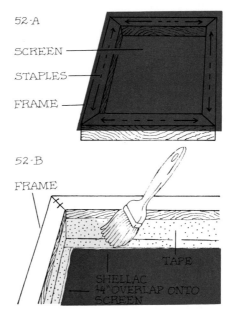

52-A
SCREEN
STAPLES
FRAME

52-B
FRAME
TAPE
SHELLAC
¼″ OVERLAP ONTO SCREEN

INKS AND DYES FOR SILKSCREEN

Since both water and oil-base stencils are used for silkscreen, inks and dyes used for this printing process must also be both water and oil-base. Water-base dyes and inks are used with oil-base stencils, and vice versa, to prevent stencils from dissolving during printing. Both types of dye and ink may be used on garments since they are eventually heat-treated for permanence. Sources for these dyes and inks appear on page 78.

FABRIC SELECTION AND PREPARATION

Natural fibers such as wool, cotton, silk, and viscose rayon absorb most

dye pigments best. Synthetic fabrics may also be silkscreened with special inks and dyes formulated just for that purpose. For either type of dye or ink, though, it is wise to print and process a sample on fabric scraps first before printing on your good fabric.

Wash, dry, and iron all fabric before printing to remove any sizing and to preshrink the cloth. If you're printing on a fabric you've dyed, make sure the dye has set completely and will not run.

Select a simple garment pattern with as few construction requirements as possible; in this case we've suggested a long A-line skirt and a simple, unlined pinafore pocket. Make any pattern alterations before cutting out the fabric; then cut out individual pattern pieces according to pattern layout and instructions. Garment construction will be done *after* all pattern pieces have been printed.

PRINTING ON FABRIC

Working on an even, flat surface, make a slightly cushioned printing base by taping several layers of newsprint to the table surface (also see page 50).

Once you're satisfied with your test scrap, tightly tape fabric pattern pieces over newsprint padding, positioning area to be printed over center of pad. Decide where designs will be positioned and mark placement for screen frame on fabric with masking tape (fig. 55-A). This creates a guide for successive color applications.

Once the screen is in place, pour dye or ink along one short side of the screen. Press the screen firmly down on the fabric and weight frame with bricks; then slowly and evenly, with some pressure, pull the dye or ink all the way across the screen with the squeegee from one short side of the frame to the other. Next push ink back to its original position and cover any dry spots in the design with a second pass over the screen with the ink and squeegee. Some designs and fabrics will require as many as 4 passes for a good print.

When finished, lift the screen *straight up* off the fabric to avoid smearing the applied color, and set fabric aside to dry. Continue until all prints to be made with this screen have been done; then remove ink and stencil from screen with solvents (ink and dye instructions will include information on the correct solvents to use).

If multicolor printing is being done, adhere stencil for next color when screen is dry. Allow fabric pieces to dry completely before printing additional colors. Repeat the above printing process for each of the remaining colors to be screened. Process the finished prints according to the instructions accompanying your dye or ink, but don't wash the printed fabric until the garment has been sewn.

SKIRT DESIGN WITH CUT-FILM STENCIL

You'll need: 1 square yard lacquer stencil film; stencil knife; cotton rags; lacquer solvent; masking tape and strips of heavy paper; commercial long A-line skirt pattern with fabric pattern pieces cut from buff-color natural fabric; water-base silkscreen inks, dyes, or textile paints in dark brown, primary blue, and coral rust; 15 by 20″ silkscreen; squeegee.

1. Enlarge pattern on page 54 to correct size; then tape enlarged design to smooth, flat surface.
2. Cut a piece of lacquer film 2″ wider and 2″ longer than design. Center film, lacquer side *up*, over design and tape into place.
3. After practicing with stencil knife on a scrap of film, carefully cut around stem, leaves, and flower bases of pattern. Cut only through film, leaving plastic backing intact.
4. Carefully peel cut lacquer film from areas you wish to print, leaving clear plastic exposed.
5. Follow steps 2 through 4 for each screen: leaves, stems, and flower bases (brown); outer flower petals (blue); and inner flower petals (rust).
6. Adhere your first stencil to screen by laying it lacquer side *up* on a clean, flat surface. Remove any dust from stencil; then center screen over stencil, silk side *down*. Weight frame with bricks.
7. Using 2 rags—one soaked in lacquer solvent, the other dry—work from center of screen outward. Moisten a small area with damp rag; then dry by rubbing it with dry rag.

Continue to dampen and dry in this manner, slightly melting stencil into screen. The stencil will become darker when adhered.
8. When entire stencil is adhered, allow screen to dry before peeling off plastic backing. If lacquer also lifts up, reapply solvent until stencil is completely adhered.
9. Block off outside margins of back and front of screen with masking tape, heavy paper strips, or contact paper (fig. 55-B).
10. Prepare fabric, and print as described on page 52. Space each print evenly around skirt hem to allow for 4 complete designs. Leave room along skirt bottom for a 3″ hem.
11. When first screen is completed, remove paint and lacquer film with appropriate solvents. Rinse off screen and allow to dry before adhering next piece of cut film (outer flower petals), following steps 6 through 9. Repeat for 3rd piece of film. Use the slight discoloration present on screen from 1st color printing as a placement guide to position 2nd and 3rd films.
12. When printing is completed, process fabric to set colors according to instructions for dye, ink, or textile paint you've used.
13. Complete construction of skirt; then hand wash to remove any unset printed ink, dye, or textile paint.

PHOTOSTENCIL PINAFORE POCKET

You'll need: Several 8 by 10″ rectangles of photo stencil film (in a light-tight box) and its accompanying developer (or make up a batch of your own developer—2 parts 10-volume drugstore hydrogen peroxide to 9 parts water); an oblong glass cake pan; #2 photoflood lamp; a spray attachment for sink faucet; 10 by 12″ rectangle of black construction paper; 10 by 12″ sheet of clear glass or acrylic; 8 by 10″ sheet of frosted acetate; ink pen; India ink; masking tape; heavy paper strips; 12 by 16″ silkscreen; squeegee; blue oil-base textile dye, ink, or paint (see page 52); solvent; rags; ½ yard prewashed white homespun cotton cut into one 11 by 38″ rectangle and five 7 by 8″ rectangles; blue sewing thread; four ⅝″ white buttons; additional textile paints.

1. To make a *positive* through which to expose your film, copy pocket design with India ink onto sheet of frosted acetate. A dense, black line is essential; reapply ink if necessary and allow to dry.
2. Make your photostencil under subdued light conditions to protect film from premature exposure. Place black construction paper on table surface, and position a rectangle of photostencil film emulsion side (dull gelatin surface) *down* over it. Center acetate positive face *down* over film, and place sheet of plate glass or acrylic on top.
3. Position photoflood bulb over glass at a height equal to *diagonal* measurement of film positive. Turn on lamp and expose for about 5 minutes.
4. While waiting, mix up your developer. Instructions for commercial developer are on package. For hydrogen peroxide and water mixture, measure enough into a glass bowl to make a 1½ to 2″-deep bath in glass tray. After developer has been mixed in a large bowl, allow any undissolved particles to settle to bottom before pouring off clear developer into tray. *This step is essential.*
5. Turn off photoflood; set aside paper and positive. Develop film by placing it in tray with developer and gently agitating for 1½ to 3 minutes.
6. Place bottom of clear glass or acrylic sheet in sink and lean it against sink wall. Lay film emulsion side *up* on this slanted surface and bathe it with a fine spray of lukewarm water. All unexposed film will wash away, leaving a negative of your acetate positive. When image is sharp, rinse with cold water to set film.
7. Place film emulsion side *up* on a newsprint-cushioned surface and center screen over film. With silk side *down*, place screen straight down on emulsion. Carefully blot away any excess water, using soft rags over newspaper. Do not blot film.
8. Allow screen to dry naturally for 1 hour or more; then slowly peel away plastic backing. If emulsion pulls away from screen, stop and allow film to dry completely before trying to remove backing a 2nd time.
9. Block out screen around stencil with masking tape and heavy paper (refer to fig. 55-B).
10. To print pockets, follow instructions on page 52.

⌐1 ⅛"⌐

Silkscreen Ideas

Subtle overall silkscreened patterns grace this superbly cut silk chiffon evening jacket. Fabric: Malorie Nelson, Riga Prints. Evening jacket design: Holly Harp.

An unusual viscose fabric, the material for this bias-cut dress and shawl is stencil-painted by airbrush with a pattern of giant peonies. Design: Frances Butler.

Initially silkscreened as one large, flat piece, this Japanese acrobat-decorated dress is similar in cut to the Mid-Eastern Caftan design on page 11. Design: Frances Butler.

11. When finished, clean ink from screen with solvent; then remove stencil from screen by soaking it in warm water for 10 minutes. Use a stiff brush to scrub away emulsion.

12. Process printed fabric according to instructions accompanying dye or ink chosen.

13. To make pinafore, follow diagram at right. After cutting out the pinafore, make an 8 by 10″ facing for neck opening and, centering it on the pinafore body, pin it in place, wrong side *up.* Sew; then iron facing to inside and iron under raw edge. Topstitch ¼″ from neck edge. Fold and iron under raw edges along both long sides of pinafore. Topstitch along sides ¼″ in from edges. Zigzag over raw edges, then turn up a 2″ hem front and back, and topstitch. Sew on buttons; then make side tabs (fig. 55-C). Iron edges under; then topstitch pocket to center front of pinafore.

14. To enliven pocket, how about coloring in areas of design with textile paints? Choose your child's favorite colors to make the design an original.

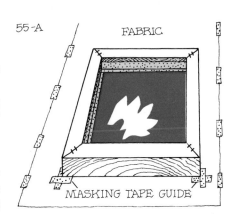

55-A

FABRIC

MASKING TAPE GUIDE

55-B

PAPER TAPED OVER EDGE OF SCREEN AS A BLOCK-OUT

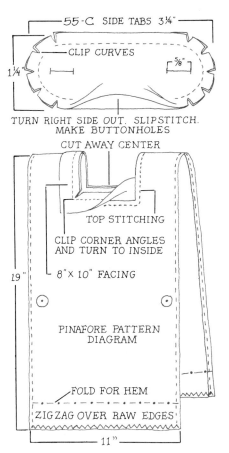

55-C SIDE TABS 3¼″

CLIP CURVES

1¼″   ⅝″

TURN RIGHT SIDE OUT. SLIPSTITCH. MAKE BUTTONHOLES

CUT AWAY CENTER

TOP STITCHING

CLIP CORNER ANGLES AND TURN TO INSIDE

8″ × 10″ FACING

19″

PINAFORE PATTERN DIAGRAM

FOLD FOR HEM

ZIGZAG OVER RAW EDGES

11″

PINAFORE DESIGN (ACTUAL SIZE)

EVERY DAY HAS COME BEFORE

WINTER ⚹ SPRING ⚹ SUMMER ⚹ FALL

TODAY COULD BE THE BEST OF ALL

Ideas for Using Dyes and Paints

A

Incredibly beautiful one-of-a-kind effects can be evolved with textile dyes and paints. Here are some exceptional garments produced by the individual efforts of several advanced and professional artists. We hope you'll find here a number of ideas to emulate in your own work with paints and dyes. Other creative ideas are offered on pages 16, 17, 40, 41, and 79.

A, B. Hothouse colors dominate this strongly designed cotton evening dress, handpainted with pigments especially formulated for use on fabrics. Design: Richard Valentino. Handpainted velvet jacket edged with fish-scale-like appliqués makes use of Tibetan motifs, as does its accompanying T-shirt, an arresting focal point. Design: Karen Warford.

C, D, E, F. Patterns reminiscent of rare malachite slabs run across this body drape dyed in the ancient African bandhanna technique. Design: Melanie De Bo. Jewels: Lee and Alex. Gorgeously tie-dyed and handpainted silk chiffon caftan has simple rectangular shape and is worn over a long slip of complementary color. Design: Patsy Lowry. Soft swirls of orange, fuschia, grape and sea blue merge and blend, creating an illusion of

movement in this tie-dyed viscose rayon dress. Design: Gertrude Reagan. Bandhanna-dyed chiffon scarf becomes part of a dramatic evening ensemble. This decorative technique is related to the shibori tie-dye approach (see page 72). Design: Melanie De Bo.

G. Batiked elegance in subtle colorations gives this flowing caftan a soft sophistication. Design: Sara Lisker.

B

C D E

H. Trompe l'oeil handpainted feather and snakeskin effects of "Medicine Wheel Cape" are set off by bead-trimmed goat hair tassels. Design: K. Lee Manuel.

I, J, K. Negative and positive areas of this handpainted silk dress possess the strong visual contrasts of a Rorschach inkblot in reverse. Design: Carolyn Oberst. Handpainted China silk "wings" adorn these three woodland ladies. Hems of "wings" are hand rolled. Design: Phyllis Mufson. Elegant dye-painted shawl and skirt juxtapose subtly shaded, lifelike florals against the sudden firmness of geometric shapes. Design: Julia Hill.

F G

H

I

K

J

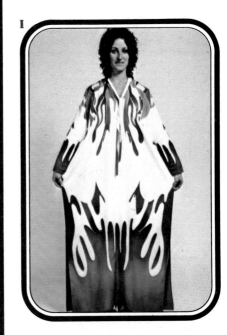

Recycling

We all play favorites with our wardrobes. Perhaps it's a pair of well-loved but worn jeans, or a sweater that fits so well we simply can't bear to part with it in spite of pulled threads and holes in its elbows.

The pity is that so many people give up so easily on these tried-and-true gems, when just a small amount of hand or machine work could turn them into special one-of-a-kind treasures too good to ever toss.

THE SECOND TIME AROUND

The concept of repairing and reusing the things we have on hand has a longer, more venerable history than the current attitude of "discard and replace." Even today, most societies make thorough use of an item before finally relegating it to the trash heap. Recycling not only makes possible the complete use of an article; it also saves a fair amount of money that would otherwise be spent to replace a broken or out-of-date item.

There is an element of challenge in the idea of taking something unwanted and using your imagination and talents to turn it into an attractive, useful article with a new lease on life. This applies especially to clothing, which, due to constant style changes, tends to go in and out of use all too quickly. So . . . recycle it. There are any number of ways to change tired old tried-and-trues into interesting, even special, additions to your current wardrobe. Some suggestions:

WAYS AND MEANS

A veritable Pandora's box of recycling ideas awaits the individual who is motivated to try them. Crochet, knitting, stitchery, patchwork, appliqué, even paints and dyes—these are just a few of the techniques that can transform blah into beautiful.

Crochet. Using only basic crochet stitches, you can add rows of a simple ruffled crochet trim down the front of a sweater; or you can repair holes in a favorite sweater by crocheting small, ruffled flowers over them (page 59).

If you're an intermediate crocheter, create long bands of a decorative crochet edging to perk up the worn collar and cuffs of a favorite shirt. Another idea: crochet and line large perle cotton granny squares or circles, then add them to a skirt, pants, or jacket as colorful pockets or as patches for worn areas.

Those of you who are advanced crocheters might renovate an old T-shirt, as we have done on page 67, by crocheting a lacy perle cotton edging with shoulder straps to change the T-shirt into a delicate camisole top.

Knitting. Like crochet, knitting can be put to a variety of uses. Left with partial balls of yarn from other projects? Knit them up into a cheerful, multicolor pullover in simple knit and purl sequence. Or use the extra yarn to create patches or a sweater pocket like that in the project on page 61. Working with larger needles or bulkier yarns, you can produce square modules of the same pattern to piece together into a confetti-bright jacket.

Other knitting ideas include unraveling old knitted garments and reusing the yarn in new projects; knitting small motifs, such as flowers or geometric shapes, and applying them to a sweater having worn spots or holes; or, if just portions of a knit garment are worth saving, sew a close zigzag stitch around the good area, cut it out (keeping the cutting line outside of the stitching to prevent raveling), and use it with other knits to make a pillow.

Stitchery. Agility with needles and threads can give you the means to redeem even the lowliest of garment rejects, as you can see by the projects presented on pages 63, 75, and 77. Even your sewing machine can get into the act, satin stitching rows and curves of bright color to the many pockets of a denim skirt (page 69).

If you master even a few embroidery stitches, you'll have the ability to make something dramatic out of something drab. Try embroidering one of your child's drawings onto a sweater. Then cover up tears or holes worn in your jeans, pants, or shirts with embroidered patches appliquéd over the holes. Another idea: use the Russian punchwork technique described on page 32 to conceal stains or worn spots on a favorite garment.

Patchwork. Here's your chance to use up those odds and ends of sewing fabric and those partially worn garments you've been hesitant to throw away because the fabric was so pretty. Work them up into traditional quilt blocks, then piece the blocks together into your own original yardage from which a spectacular skirt and shirt set can be cut and sewn.

Or make yourself a padded jacket from the pattern on page 13 by cutting the basic pattern apart into a number of smaller pieces. Add a seam allowance to each piece, cut adjoining pieces from various fabrics, and sew them all up into a complete jacket pattern piece to be padded and lined.

Applique. Use everything from ribbons, buttons, and commercial patches to your own personally created appliqués to spruce up your "closet cases." One way is to combine fusible bonding, satin stitch, and fabric scraps on your sewing machine to make up your own durable appliqués; then sew them to anything that needs patching or a pick-me-up.

Paints and dyes. Take our advice and give the dyed T-shirt and painted jeans projects on pages 72 and 73 a try. You'll be amazed how a bit of extra color can add zip to just about anything. And it's really so easy.

Try some simple tie-dye to perk up an old skirt or blouse; just tie overhand knots all over the garment and dye. When the knots come out—sunbursts! Specifics on dyes and paints are given on page 43.

Note: For information on transferring designs, please refer to page 24.

Recycling

Crocheted flowers repair a torn sweater (below), and a knitted pocket adds new life to an old sweater (right). Directions for flower appliqués are on page 60. Design: Pamela Hinchcliffe. Directions for pocket are on page 61. Design: Marika Contompasis.

Idea:

Simple sleeves composed of compelling pattern repeats and a Peruvian-inspired portrait of the sweater's owner enhance the shape of this crocheted sweater. Design: Linda Mendelson.

Floral Crochet Sweater Appliqués

COLOR PHOTO ON PAGE 59

Wearing or tearing a hole in your favorite sweater needn't be a real disaster. Turn tragedy into triumph by crocheting these spritely floral accents to cover the gaps. The flowers and leaves, all done in single crochet, are easy and quick to work up. If you're mending a woolen sweater, use wool worsted yarns; if the sweater yarn is synthetic, use a manmade fiber. Crochet abbreviations are explained on page 67.

You'll need: 2 oz. fine worsted wool or synthetic yarn in *each* of 2 coordinated colors (choose shades that either harmonize or contrast with the sweater) for flowers and in 1 shade of green for leaves; #1 or #00 crochet hook; scissors; large-eye tapestry needle.

1. Clip off any hanging yarn ends; then start flower by working 14 ch st into sweater yarn surrounding hole (fig. 60-A-B), catching loose loops of sweater yarn to prevent them from "running." Join with sl st, ch 1.

2. Row 2: Dec all around (to dec: make 7 sc dec, one for every 2 st of the 14 ch st). Sl st at end; ch 1. You now have 7 st all around.

AS IN THIS FACSIMILE YOUR FLOWER PATCHES CAN CHANGE COLORS. ADD A LEAF FOR AN EXTRA TOUCH.

3. Row 3: 3 sc in each sc all around; sl st.

4. Row 4: 2 sc in each sc all around; sl st. Flower should be ruffling at this point.

5. Row 5: Change yarn color but do not inc; do 1 sc in each sc all around flower and sl st at end. For larger flowers, add more rows as in Step 4 before changing yarn color for edging. Attached flower is now completed. For bouquet effect, begin other flowers using base of first flower as an anchor. Crochet as in steps 1 through 5.

6. To crochet leaf, ch 6; sk 1st ch, sc in next 4 ch, 3 sc in last ch. Picking up other side of ch, sc in next 4 sc. 3 sc at end. ch 6; sk 1st ch, 3 sc in last ch. Picking up other side of ch: 4 sc. 3 sc at end to make leaf shape into an oblong.

7. Do 3 or 4 more rows of sc all around until leaf is desired size (inc at ends if necessary to prevent puckering); sl st at end to join.

8. Use tapestry needle and green yarn to sew leaf down to sweater. Tuck 1 end of leaf under flower and anchor; then work out along edges of leaf to tip. Knot yarn inside of sweater to secure.

60-A   60-B

TO START

WORK ALL REMAINING ch st IN FIRST rnd IN THIS MANNER

Knitted Pocket Pick-me-up

COLOR PHOTO ON PAGE 59

If you're an intermediate knitter, you can perk up a tired sweater with this handknitted, multicolored Chinese motif patch pocket. Colors are carried over on the back of this silk-lined, knitted square, which is worked from the color-coded graph below. The silk trim is handstitched over the edges of the knit, then carefully tacked to the sweater.

You'll need: 1 pr. #1 knitting needles; one 1-oz. skein of 3-ply wool fingering yarn in *each* of the following colors: white, dark blue, light blue, red, and purple; 5 yarn bobbins; scissors; ¼ yard blue silk lining; blue sewing thread; needle; ruler; straight pins; 10 by 10″ soft wood board or pressboard; an old sweater.

1. Wind ½ oz. of each color onto yarn bobbins; then cast on 56 stitches with red yarn.
2. To knit pocket, refer to graph below. Stitch gauge on #1 needles is 8 stitches per inch horizontally and 12 rows per inch vertically. *Each* vertical row of squares on graph equals *2 rows* of stitches; each horizontal row of squares equals 1 individual stitch

61-A BEGINNING COLOR CHANGES

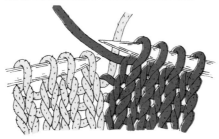

61-B TRADING OFF COLORED YARNS

per square. Begin working from lower right corner across to left corner; for second row, work from left to right. Repeat sequence for entire graph.
3. When coming to a color change, pick up new color behind and underneath old color (fig. 61-A). Twist old and new strands once around one another, and then proceed with new color (fig. 61-B). Carry unused threads with you as you knit the row, and secure these "floats" each time a new color is begun. Repeat this step for each color change.
4. When square is completed, bind off. Trace an 8 by 8″ square onto a piece of soft wood; then dampen knitted square and pin its edges down in alignment with drawn square. Allow knitting to dry; then remove pins.
5. Cut a 10 by 10″ square of silk lining. Fold under ½″ all around and press to crease. Fold under another ½″ all around and press. Lay knit square over lining and bring folded edges up over edges of knit square. Pin into place and slipstitch (see page 8) lining to pocket.
6. Center pocket on front of sweater and pin down; then slipstitch sides and bottom into place.

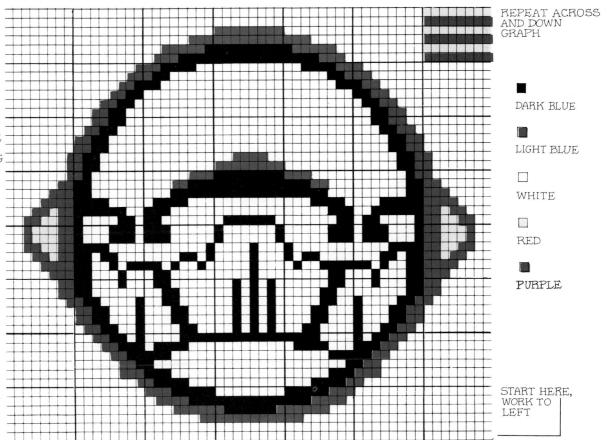

GAUGE:
1 INCH
EQUALS
12 VERTICAL
ROWS

1 INCH
EQUALS
8 HORIZONAL
STITCHES

EACH SQUARE
EQUALS ONE
STITCH GOING
ACROSS
GRAPH, AND
TWO ROWS
GOING UP
GRAPH

REPEAT ACROSS
AND DOWN
GRAPH

■ DARK BLUE

▨ LIGHT BLUE

□ WHITE

□ RED

▦ PURPLE

START HERE,
WORK TO
LEFT

Recycling

A trio of good ideas: Button collector's shirt (top, right) makes new use of old buttons. Directions are on page 63. Design: Marilyn Bauriedel. Jogger's sweatshirt slogan is sewn from scraps of felt and embroidery floss. Directions are on page 64. Design: Gail Newton. Yarn-decorated sweater has leftover yarn ends latch-hooked to its sleeves. Directions are on page 65. Design: Marilyn Bauriedel.

Buttoned-up Shirt

COLOR PHOTO ON PAGE 62

When you think of recycling, think about other reusables besides clothing. Buttons are much more fun when they're out and about, instead of cooped up in a canister or box. Get an extra bonus from your button collection by using it to add some spice to a shirt or jacket.

If your collection doesn't consist of 300 blue, green, brown, and white buttons as ours does, just design your own shirt decoration sized to accommodate your cache of colorful buttons. Remember—you can always use the buttons over again when the shirt wears out.

You'll need: Long-sleeved and cuffed brown boy's shirt, size 7; 300 small and medium-size buttons (more for a larger shirt) in the following color groupings: 20 white, 100 assorted blues, 120 assorted greens, 20 beige, 30 assorted browns, and 10 multicolored; 1 spool sewing thread in *each* of the following colors: white, blue, green, and brown; 1 skein orange cotton embroidery floss; 1 skein *each* of green and white perle

63-A RUNNING

cotton embroidery thread; scissors; crewel embroidery needle; sewing needle.

1. Sew 2 parallel lines of running stitches (fig. 63-A) across front of shirt from underarm to underarm, using orange embroidery floss.
2. Enlarge pattern above (see page 24) and transfer to right shirt front above running lines. For left shirt front

design, flop pattern over and transfer so it is the mirror image of right shirt front design.
3. Outline dinosaur shapes with 2 rows of couching in green perle cotton thread (see page 77).
4. Divide buttons into basic color groups; then divide color groups into dark, medium, and light-colored piles.
5. Following pattern outlines on shirt front and color guides given in drawing below, start to sew colored buttons onto corresponding pattern areas. Three or four double-thread stitches through the holes of each button are

enough to secure it. When working inside of a couched area, try to keep edges of buttons within couching.
6. When both shirt front panels are completed, divide remaining buttons into 2 equal groups, mixing colors and button shapes. Sew buttons to shirt cuffs, varying placement and colors of buttons.
7. Embroider dinosaur's eyes with 3 French knots (fig. 63-B).
8. Always wash this shirt by hand in warm water.

63-B FRENCH KNOT

3/4"

WHITE BUTTONS

BLUE BUTTONS

WHITE BUTTONS

GREEN BUTTONS

GREEN BUTTONS

GREEN BUTTONS

TAN BUTTONS

BROWN BUTTONS

Jogger's Novelty Sweatshirt

COLOR PHOTO ON PAGE 62

"Take good care of your body today . . ."—the family jogging fan will get a kick out of this project and so will you. Everything (except the felt letters) has been recycled from existing garments and fabric scraps like those you probably have.

You'll need: 1 pair worn-out jeans sized for an 8 to 10-year-old; medium-size grey sweatshirt; ¼ yard felt in *each* of the following colors (or use 1 felt square approximately 8 by 10″ for each word): gold, turquoise, magenta, dark brown, purple, red, and black; ¼ yard denim or corduroy print (any color); ¼ yard black and white gingham check cotton; 1 spool of thread to match *each* of the felt colors; 1½ yards decorative wide bias seam tape (any color); 1 collared shirt pattern in same size range as sweatshirt; pins; scissors; ruler; pencil; paper; zigzag sewing machine.

1. Draw a line on each jeans leg 10½ to 11½″ above cuff; cut off each leg at marked line. Cut legs off lower, if necessary, to avoid any existing holes.
2. Draw a line on each sweatshirt sleeve 10 to 11″ above wrist; cut off sleeves at marked line. If pieces from jean legs are shorter than 10½ to 11½″, adjust sleeve cut-off accordingly; sleeves are always cut ½″ less than jeans leg measurement.
3. Turn 1 leg piece inside out and slide it over cut-off end of 1 sleeve. Match and pin raw edges; then sew together with a ½″ seam (fig. 64-A). Turn sleeve right side out and fold seam towards body. Topstitch seam in place with red zigzag stitching. Repeat procedure for other sleeve.
4. Measure 2″ down from sweatshirt neck opening and mark off points all around neck. Connect points to form a circular cutting line. Cut along this line and discard original crew neck.
5. Slash center front neck to a point 1½″ below cut edge.
6. Cut a 30″-long bias strip from part

of jeans remaining after legs were removed (strip can be pieced if necessary). Right sides facing, pin then sew 1 edge of bias strip to cut neck edge of sweatshirt. Begin sewing at 1 side of 1½″-long slash in center front and continue around neck to end at other side of slash. Press seam toward neck opening and topstitch into place.
7. Cut a 2 by 4″ piece of sweatshirt fabric from discarded sleeve; right sides facing, use it to bind edges of neck slash and bias strip (fig. 64-B). Turn to inside and press under a ¼″ seam. Overcast (fig. 64-C).
8. Using commercial pattern as marking and cutting guide, cut out collar from gingham check fabric; cut out facing from corduroy or denim print fabric. Follow pattern directions to make collar; then set aside.
9. Gather upper edge of neck bias strip until it matches size of collar-base opening; then tie off gathering threads to secure. Attach collar to gathered neck edge, following commercial pattern directions. For strength, topstitch along collar base.
10. Cut off waistband of sweatshirt and, right sides facing, sew on a strip of wide bias tape. Iron seam towards shirt body and topstitch into place.

Fold bias tape to inside so that ¼″ shows below topstitched lower edge. Pin tape in place and overcast.
11. Enlarge lettering to correct size (see page 24) and make paper patterns. Pin patterns to appropriate felt squares and cut out letters. Arrange letters on front of sweatshirt and pin. Machine zigzag over edges of letters with matching thread to secure.

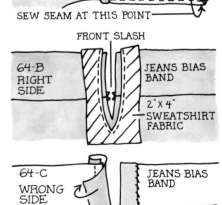

Yarn Confetti Sweater

COLOR PHOTO ON PAGE 62

Anyone who knits, crochets, weaves, or makes baskets or hooked rugs usually finds leftover yarn on hand at the end of a project—not really enough yarn to make a complete item, but too much to throw away with an easy conscience.

If you're a member of this group, consider a suggestion you may not have thought of for using up those extra bits and pieces of yarn: latch hook them into an old bulky, loose-knit, or crocheted sweater. You can make an entire garment into a warm, closely packed jacket; or, as we have done, use the technique to spruce up a still useful, but plain sweater.

You'll need: Standard rug latch hook; various yarns in either white, turquoise, steel blue, green, and deep blue or from your stock of leftovers (since knit gauges and sweater sizes will vary for this project, no specific amounts of yarn can be indicated); scissors; 3″ square of heavy cardboard; pencil; scissors; old sweater.

1. As in figure 65-A, use 3″ square of cardboard to wind and cut your yarn into 3″ lengths. Avoid stretching yarn as you wrap. Group yarns by colors.
2. To learn use of a latch hook, see figure 65-B. Begin to work at underarm seam of one sleeve of sweater, using 1 strand for each hole if working with thick yarns. If you also have thin yarns, though, bunch them into a bundle and latch them as 1 strand; this will give you an opportunity to mix in some subtle color variations.
3. Follow figure 65-C for color placement. All colors are worked in rows around sleeve from shoulder seam down toward elbow. When 1 sleeve is done, repeat for 2nd sleeve.

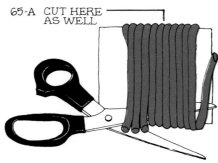

65-A CUT HERE AS WELL

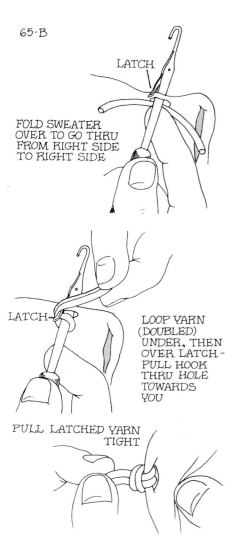

65-B

LATCH

FOLD SWEATER OVER TO GO THRU FROM RIGHT SIDE TO RIGHT SIDE

LATCH

LOOP YARN (DOUBLED) UNDER, THEN OVER LATCH—PULL HOOK THRU HOLE TOWARDS YOU

PULL LATCHED YARN TIGHT

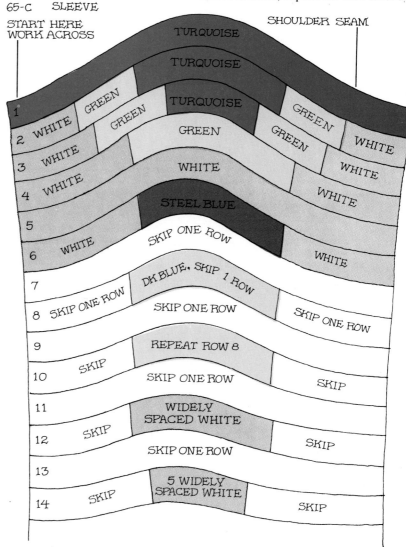

65-C SLEEVE

START HERE WORK ACROSS

SHOULDER SEAM

Row					
1		GREEN	TURQUOISE		
2	WHITE	GREEN	TURQUOISE	GREEN	WHITE
3	WHITE		GREEN	GREEN	WHITE
4	WHITE		WHITE		WHITE
5			STEEL BLUE		
6	WHITE	SKIP ONE ROW			WHITE
7		DK BLUE, SKIP 1 ROW			
8	SKIP ONE ROW	SKIP ONE ROW		SKIP ONE ROW	
9	SKIP	REPEAT ROW 8			
10		SKIP ONE ROW		SKIP	
11	SKIP	WIDELY SPACED WHITE			
12		SKIP ONE ROW		SKIP	
13	SKIP	5 WIDELY SPACED WHITE			
14				SKIP	

Recycling

Two-tone Crochet-Trimmed Camisole Top, made from an old T-shirt, and machine embroidered and appliquéd skirt of old denim pockets are a smart combination. Directions for camisole top begin on page 67. Design: Nancy Lawton. Directions for pocket skirt are on page 69. Design: Suki Diamond.

Idea:

One by one, the crocheted motifs of this jacket were spontaneously created by the artist in a silk/cotton blend of floss, then finally joined from back to front to produce a spectacular fitted jacket. Design: Maggie Kouwenberg.

Crochet-trimmed Camisole Top

COLOR PHOTO ON PAGE 66

If you crochet, you'll find this unique camisole top a treat to make and wear. The trim is first crocheted as one continuous piece, then sewn to a soft cotton T-shirt body that can be either cut down from an old white T-shirt or made from cotton knit fabric.

Either way, choose a 100 percent cotton fabric, because the top will be dyed in a single dyebath of scarlet. The shirt's two-tone appearance after dyeing results from the use of materials with two different fiber densities.

Information on dyes can be found on page 43. The top is sized small, medium, and large; the numbers inside the parentheses apply to medium and large sizes, respectively.

You'll need: Large ball white perle cotton; old white T-shirt in a medium or large size or ½ yard of 45''-wide white 100 percent cotton knit fabric; red thread; 4 stitch markers (see step 1); #6 steel crochet hook; tape measure; pins; 1 packet scarlet red dye and related ingredients and equipment called for on packet.

1. Make 4 stitch markers by taping short strips of masking tape to 4 me-dium safety pins (fig. 67-A). Number tags 1, 2, 3, and 4.

2. *Base chain* (see fig. 67-B): Ch 80 (88, 96) for back; place marker #1. Ch 100 (108, 116) for lft underarm; place marker #2. Ch 80 (88, 96) for front; place marker #3. Ch 100 (108, 116) for rgt underarm; place marker #4. Being careful not to twist ch, join with sl st to 1st ch.

3. *Shell edging:* From marker #4, sk st, 4 hdc in next st, sk st, sl st in next st (one complete shell pattern made). Work 20 (22, 24) shells to #1, 25 (27, 29) shells to #2, 20 (22, 24) shells to #3, and 25 (27, 29) shells to #4, ending with sl st.

4. *Shoulder straps:* Ch 92 (100, 108) for rgt shoulder strap; taking care not to twist, join with sl st to #3 (see fig. 70-B). Sl st in 1st hdc to lft of #3 to secure. Work 23 (25, 27) shells to #4, ending with sl st. Sl st in 1st hdc to rgt of #4 to secure. Cut and weave in end. Insert needle and draw up thread at #4. Sl st in 1st hdc on opposite side of #4 to secure. Work back to #3, making 1 shell in back of each shell, and sl st in back of each sl st. Sl st in hdc to rgt of #3 to secure. End off. Repeat this step between markers #1 and #2 for 2nd strap.

5. *Rnd 1:* Working along base ch (straight edge of shells), insert hook opposite middle of 13th (14th, 15th) shell between #1 and #2 (middle of lft underarm), pick up thread, ch 1. * Sc in each st until 1st shell before marker #1. Sc in 1st st of shell, in next st (center of shell) draw up loop, in st at #1 draw up loop, in center st of next shell draw up loop (4 loops on hook), yo, draw through all 4 loops (corner made). Repeat from * all around, working sc in each st, and working corner at each marker. Join with sl st to 1st ch in rnd.

6. *Rnd 2:* Ch 4 (counts as 1st dc, ch 1). * Sk st, dc in top of next st, ch 1. Continue same around (dc's should be opposite center st and sl sts of shells). Dc center of 2nd shell before corner, do not ch, dc in center of 2nd shell after corner. Continue from * until passing #3 and completing 18 (20, 22) dc. Ch 4, sl st in top of 18th (20th, 22nd) dc to form loop (center front), ch 1. Continue working dc, ch 1 around as described above. Sl st in 3rd ch of 1st ch 4 to join.

7. *Rnd 3:* Ch 4. * Dc in top of dc of last rnd, ch 1. Continue from * stopping with dc 2 sps (not counting corner sp) before corner. 3 tr into large corner sp leaving last loop on hook each time (4 loops on hook), yo, draw through all 4 loops. Dc in 3rd dc from corner sp, ch 1. Continue from * stopping with dc preceding center front loop of previous rnd. 7 tr in loop, dc in next dc, ch 1. Continue same all around. Sl st in 3rd ch of ch 4 to join.

8. *Rnd 4:* Sc in next sp of previous rnd, * ch 3, sc (scallop made). Continue from * ending with sc in 3rd sp from corner (3 dc remaining). 4 tr in corner st, ch 4, sl st in top of last tr made to form loop, 3 more tr in same corner st. Sk 3 dc, sc in 3rd sp, ch 3. Repeat from * ending with sc when there are 2 dc remaining before center front. Ch 2, 4 tr in top of 2nd tr of last rnd, ch 4, sl st in top of last tr

CROCHET KEY

ch: chain
dc: double crochet
dec: decrease
hdc: half double crochet
inc: increase
lft: left
rgt: right
rnd: round
sc: single crochet
sk st(s): skip stitch(es)
sl st(s): slip stitch(s)
sp(s): space(s)
st(s): stitch(es)
tr: triple crochet
X: times (as in 3X's = 3 times)
yo: yarn over
*: repeat information from asterisk as many times as noted
( ): repeat information in parentheses as many times as specified

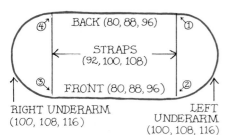

67-A

67-B

BACK (80, 88, 96)

STRAPS (92, 100, 108)

FRONT (80, 88, 96)

RIGHT UNDERARM (100, 108, 116)

LEFT UNDERARM (100, 108, 116)

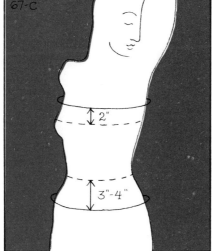

67-C

2"

3"-4"

made to form loop, 3 more tr into same st. Ch 1, sk st, tr in next st, ch 4, sl st in top of last tr made to form loop. Ch 1, sk st, 4 tr in next st, ch 4, sl st in top of last tr made to form loop, 3 more tr in same st. Ch 2, sk 2 dc, sc in next sp, ch 3. Repeat from * all around, ending with sl st in 1st sc at beginning of rnd.

9. *Rnd 5:* Work as in Rnd 4, ending with sc in last ch 3 sp before corner. Ch 2, 4 dc in loop, ch 2, sc in next ch 3 sp. Continue scallops and corners as established, ending with sc in last ch 3 sp before center front (ch 2, 5 dc in next loop) 3 X's, ch 2, sc in next sp. Continue with scallops all around, working corner as above, ending with sl st as in Rnd 4.

10. *Rnd 6:* Work as in Rnd 4, ending with sc, ch 3 in last ch 3 sp before corner. At corner in sp between 1st and 2nd dc, work 3 tr leaving last loop on hook each time (4 loops on hook), yo, draw through all 4 loops (petal made), ch 3. (Work petal in next sp, ch 3) 2 X's. Sc in next scallop sp. Repeat scallops and corners as established, ending with sc in last scallop before center front. Ch 3, (work petal, ch 3, petal, ch 3, petal, ch 4, evenly spaced along cluster of 5 dc) 2 X's. Work (petal, ch 3,) 3 X's over last cluster of 5 dc. Sc in next scallop. Continue scallops and corners as established, ending with sl st as in Rnd 4.

11. *Rnd 7:* Work as in Rnd 4, ending with sc in last scallop before corner. (Sc in tip of petal, ch 5) 2 X's, sc in petal, sc in next scallop. Repeat scallops and corners as established, ending with sc in last scallop before center front. Ch 2, sc in tip of petal. (Ch 5, sc in petal) 8 X's. Ch 2, sc in next scallop. Work scallops and corner to complete rnd, ending with sl st as in Rnd 4.

12. *Rnd 8:* Work as in Rnd 4, ending with sc in last scallop before corner, ch 3, sc in ch 5 sp of previous rnd. Ch 3, sc in sc, ch 3, sc in ch 5 sp, ch 3, sc in scallop. Repeat scallops and corners as established, ending with sc in last scallop before center front. Ch 3, (sk ch 2 sp), sc in sc, ch 3, sc in ch 5 sp, ch 3, sc in sc. Continue around center front working scallops in this manner, ending with sc in last sc, ch 3, (sk ch 2 sp), sc in next scallop. Work scallops and corner to complete rnd. End off.

13. Lightly steam-press crochet trim into shape; then try it on and measure around your chest at point where bottom edge of crochet falls, and around top of your hips (a point 3″ to 4″ below your waist). Next, measure length from 2″ above chest measurement to 1½″ below hip measurement (fig. 67-C).

14. Cut a rectangle of cotton knit fabric (either from old T-shirt or yardage) to these specifications: width should be 1″ to 2″ *smaller* (fabric will stretch) than your chest or hip measurement (whichever is larger), and length should be as measured (i.e., 2″ above chest measurement to 1½″ below hip measurement).

15. Folding fabric right sides facing, and leaving ¼″ seam allowance, sew down side seam; then turn tube right side out. Divide 1 open end of tube into 4 equal parts and mark with pins as follows: from side seam to center front, center front to side, side to back center, and back center to side seam.

16. Repeat for crochet trim; then pin trim *over* top edge of tube with wrong side of crochet to right side of fabric tube; match pins carefully. Crochet will probably be larger than tube; if so, ease crochet scallops into deeper curves to fit fabric width.

17. Sew twice along bottom of crochet scallops to attach trim to tube. Trim away excess fabric to a ¼″ seam. Turn up ¾″ hem along bottom edge of tube and hemstitch over raw edge.

18. To dye completed top, prepare dye according to package directions for dyeing cotton. Wet tank top thoroughly; then submerge it in dyebath. Circulate dye and frequently move tank top around in dyebath to assure even dyeing. When top is a shade darker than desired, remove from dyebath, rinse, and allow top to dry.

Crochet Ideas

Charming crocheted dress, made in sections, includes multicolored ruffles, medallions, even a face. Design: Maria de Conceição.

Multicolored coat, crocheted of successive geometric border designs, is topped with popcorn stitches. Design: Pam Hinchcliffe.

"Phoenix Coat," crocheted in a jagged stripe pattern, unbuttons along arms and sides to lie flat. Design: Marika Contompasis.

Patch Pocket Skirt

COLOR PHOTO ON PAGE 66

Certainly one of the most amusing "carryalls" around, this old denim skirt is covered from top to bottom with pockets made of scraps of old denim and existing jeans pockets. Machine zigzag, blind hem, and straight stitches careen across each pocket in colorful freeform style, while star studs and machine appliqué add individual touches of whimsy.

You'll need: Old denim skirt; 16 denim back pockets (extras can be made from legs of old denims); two 14 by 20″ scraps of denim (for curved front pockets); 1 package *each* of large and medium gold star studs; 1 gold heart stud; 2 spools cotton sewing thread in *each* of the following colors: red (1), lt. yellow (2), dark yellow (3), brown (4), green (5), light blue (6), dark blue (7), maroon (8), and purple (9); 2 spools gold metallic thread (10) (or equivalent color of sewing thread); assorted rickrack and ribbon (11); assorted floral printed fabric; zigzag sewing machine; scissors; pins; ruler; white chalk

1. Remove old pockets from jeans. If there aren't enough pockets, make extras from denim scraps by tracing around an existing pocket and adding a ⅝″ seam allowance all around before cutting out new pocket.
2. To make 2 large curved patch pockets, enlarge curved pocket pattern (right). Pin pattern to the two 12 by 18″ scraps (laid face to face) and trace, adding ⅝″ seams all around before cutting.
3. Enlarge stitching designs above freehand and trace onto pockets.
4. Machine embroidery varies from satin zigzag stitch set at 15 to 20 stitches per inch and ¼″ in width to freeform straight stitch worked with feed dogs down and low presser foot pressure. Consult your sewing machine manual for correct decorative stitch settings and procedures for your machine, or see page 28. Use the

photo on page 66 and number key below, left as a color guide.
5. To use metallic thread, wind it onto your machine bobbin by hand. Loosen bobbin tension slightly until

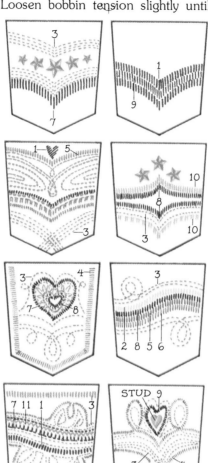

STITCHING DESIGNS

thread runs easily. Then sew with your fabric *face down* so bobbin thread appears on face of fabric.
6. When all sewn designs are completed, add any rickrack or braid trims desired and attach appropriate studs, following package directions.
7. For machine appliqué at center of skirt front, cut out floral print from fabric and baste or bond into place (pocket will be sewn on later). Satin zigzag stitch over raw edges.
8. To attach large patch pockets, turn under upper curved pocket seam and topstitch, clipping curves as needed to keep flat; then pin each pocket into place, slightly overlapping side seams and waistband. Open side and waistband seams where pockets overlap and slide pocket tops and sides into seams. Turn under curved bottom edge of each pocket, then topstitch into place, clipping curves as needed. Make a 2nd row of stitches ¼″ inside 1st row.

Next, resew side seams, catching pocket edges inside seams. Reposition waistband and topstitch back into place, catching upper pocket edges in waistband seam.
9. Turn under and topstitch upper edges of all handmade pockets; then turn under remaining seams on all pockets and iron flat. Pin pockets into position and topstitch each into place around bottom and side edges. Finish each pocket with a 2nd row of topstitching, ¼″ inside 1st row.

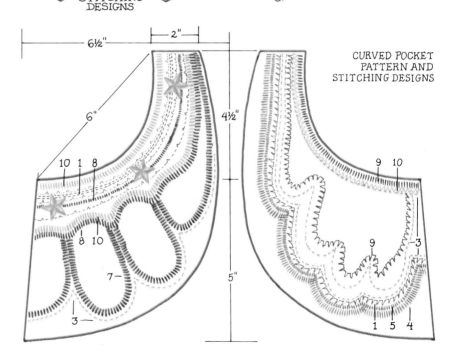

CURVED POCKET PATTERN AND STITCHING DESIGNS

Scrap Collage-trimmed Jacket

COLOR PHOTO ON PAGE 71

Scraps of bias tape, beads, buttons, and embroidery floss left over from various projects have a habit of ending up half-forgotten at the bottom of your sewing basket. Instead of leaving them to such an unproductive fate, why not put them to work decorating the Cretan Island jacket from page 20? Add a pair of patch pockets, then do beadwork, embroidery, and hand quilting as subtle accents.

You'll need: Scraps of cotton blend, single-fold bias tape in the following sizes and colors (other colors and sizes may be substituted, if you wish): 3 yards ¼″-wide brown, 2 yards ¼″-wide light blue, 3 yards ¼″-wide light tan, 3 yards ½″-wide light blue, 1 yard ½″-wide light tan, 2 yards 1″-wide tan; 1 skein *each* of embroidery floss in light blue, tan, and dark brown; 1 package *each* Indian seed beads in opaque brown and opaque light blue; 4 tan and 14 light blue ½″ buttons (or equivalent); 2 yards ⅛″-diameter cording; embroidery or quilting needle; beading needle; scissors; straight pins; paper; pencil; sewing machine; butternut and pale blue Cretan Island jacket with 7″ square patch pockets.

1. Measure around cuff of jacket from seam to seam to determine length of longest bias strips (fig. 70-A). Then cut bias tape strips in this length as follows: 2 of ¼″-wide brown, 2 of ½″-wide light blue, 2 of 1″-wide tan, 4 of ¼″-wide light tan.

Also cut 4″ to 6″ strips of bias tape as follows: 10 of ¼″-wide light blue, 4 of ¼″-wide brown. Also cut four 2″ strips of ¼″-wide brown and four 4″ strips of ¼″-wide light blue tape. For pocket decoration, cut four 7″ strips of ¼″-wide brown and two 7″ strips of ½″-wide light tan tape.

2. Start cuff decoration at a point ¼″ up from cuff edge and work upward, turning under all raw edges on tape. Begin by pinning down one continuous band of ¼″-wide light tan tape. Sew band in place with running stitches (see page 35), using a single strand of tan floss as thread. This gives the band a quilted effect.

3. The next row of bias tape is composed of alternating strips of ¼″-wide blue and brown tape in this order: 4″ long light blue, 4″ long brown, 4″ long light blue, 2″ long brown, 4″ long light blue, 2″ long brown, 4″ long light blue, 4″ long brown, and 4″ long light blue. Turn under ends of strips and adjust their lengths until they run end to end around cuff. Pin down; then hand-topstitch as in step 2 using blue floss for brown strips and brown floss for blue strips.

4. A single light tan ¼″-wide bias strip running from seam to seam of cuff makes up row 3. Pin and sew down as in step 2.

5. Repeat step 4, but use a continuous strip of ½″-wide light blue tape and topstitch with brown floss. Edge with a row of chain stitch (see page 26) in light blue floss.

6. Repeat step 4, but use a continuous strip of ¼″-wide brown tape and topstitch with blue floss.

7. Repeat step 4, using a continuous strip of 1″-wide tan tape and topstitch with tan floss.

8. To finish tape ends, pin two 4″ strips of ¼″-wide light blue tape over tape ends on both sides of seam (fig. 70-B). Topstitch with brown floss.

9. To decorate 1″-wide band of tan, make a paper circle pattern by tracing with pencil around a ½″ button, then drawing a smaller ⅜″-diameter circle centered within each larger circle. Lightly trace circles along the 1″-wide tan tape, leaving ½″ between circles. This allows for approximately 20 circles. Use a single strand of blue floss to embroider chain stitch circles over the pencilled-in patterns. Then sew running stitch circles of single-strand brown floss inside each chain-stitched circle (fig. 70-C). Along upper edge of tan tape, sew a single row of double-strand brown floss chain stitches.

10. Complete sleeve decoration by using beading needle to sew a single row of brown Indian seed beads below row of light tan tape nearest cuff edge. Also sew a single row of blue Indian seed beads above line of brown chain stitching next to 1″-wide tan band.

11. Repeat steps 2 through 10 to decorate remaining cuff.

12. To decorate pocket, start at upper edge and work downward. First, pin a 7″-long strip of ¼″-wide brown tape ⅛″ down from pocket edge and topstitch into place with single-strand blue floss, turning under both raw ends. Follow with a band of ½″-wide light tan tape sewn in place with single-strand tan floss. End with another 7″-long strip of brown tape topstitched in blue. Sew 7 blue and 2 brown buttons to ½″-wide light tan tape, spacing them evenly along tape in this order: 3 blue, 1 brown, 1 blue, 1 brown, 3 blue (fig. 70-D).

13. To complete pocket design, sew 1 row of brown Indian seed beads along top edge of pocket and 1 row of blue beads directly below bottom strip of brown tape. To finish, embroider a line of chain stitches in double-strand blue floss over machine topstitching.

14. Repeat steps 12 and 13 for remaining pocket.

70-A MEASURE FROM SEAM TO SEAM OF SLEEVE

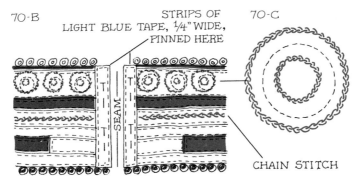

70-B STRIPS OF LIGHT BLUE TAPE, ¼″ WIDE, PINNED HERE

SEAM

70-C

CHAIN STITCH

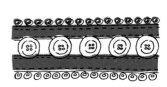

70-D POCKET DECORATION

Idea:

Guatemalan fabrics form the body of a pieced jacket trimmed with myriad braidwork and tassels; a mola-decorated shirt peeks out from underneath. Design: Yvonne Porcella.

Recycling

Collage-trimmed Cretan Jacket (above right—also see page 20) esthetically elevates leftover sewing notions to the level of art. Directions are on page 70. Design: Marilyn Green. Color coordinate this Shibori-Dyed T-Shirt (center) with a pair of Mayan Motif Painted Jeans (bottom) for an eye-catching outfit. Shibori T-shirt directions are on page 72. Design: Eleanor Garcia. Directions for painted jeans are on page 73. Design: Laura Folger.

Shibori-dyed T-shirt

COLOR PHOTO ON PAGE 71

Revitalize your aging T's with *shibori,* a formalized but simple Japanese method for tritik (sewn) tie-dye.

A specific design composed of traditional shibori motifs is stitched in the cloth with doubled thread and a sharp needle; then the thread is pulled up extra tight and knotted. This effectively "ties" off spots in the fabric which resist dye penetration and remain white throughout the dyebath process. The T-shirt is then rinsed and the stitches are removed, leaving small dotted and dashed lines.

You'll need: One 100 percent white cotton knit T-shirt; 1 spool white mercerized waxed cotton thread, size 40; 1 sharps size 7 or 8 sewing needle (or any strong, sharp, thin needle); embroidery scissors; 1 packet rust or terra cotta all-purpose hot water dye; uniodized salt; large enamel or stainless steel pan; glass measuring cup; pencil; steam iron.

1. If a new T-shirt is used, prewash in soapy water; rinse and dry.

2. Freehand, copy design at right (fig. 72-A) onto T-shirt front with pencil. To draw the 3 concentric circles, trace around spools, glasses, or jars.

3. First, thread your needle with a double length of thread and, leaving a tail, knot both ends together; then practice each shibori stitch (shown below) on a scrap of soft cloth.

4. To stitch up the shirt, refer to figure 72-A and measure lengths of design lines on shirt; measure out lengths of thread at least 4 times as long as each motif area or line section.

5. Following stitch diagram in figure 72-A, start at upper right shoulder and work down, using the Undulating Stripe motif, to tip of flower.

6. Measure from top of flower around to base of stem; thread on appropriate length of thread. Work in Undulating Stripe to base of stem.

7. Sew remainder of flower, working as in steps 5 and 6.

8. Next, sew each horizontal line in-

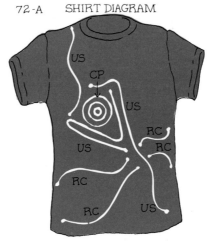

72-A   SHIRT DIAGRAM

US = UNDULATING STRIPE
RC = RESERVE CHEVRON
CP = CHINESE PINE

72-B   APPEARANCE OF GATHERED CLOTH

dividually using the Reserve Chevron motif. After every 5 or 6 stitches in first line, pull stitched line of fabric up into a tightly gathered bunch; do this until whole line is gathered before knotting off. Repeat for remaining lines.

9. Finally, sew each of folded-over concentric circles in Chinese Pine motif at center of flower, leaving 2″ to 3″ of thread at end of each circle. To gather fabric, work from center out, pulling each thread up tightly and knotting off (see below, left). At this point, start gathering cloth up along all stitched lines of thread worked so far until it is bunched tightly together (fig. 72-B); then, holding gathers together firmly, knot each thread against gathered cloth 2 or 3 times, being careful not to break threads. Leave about 2″ of thread at ends and cut off excess.

10. Make sure all shibori lines are drawn up and knotted as tightly as possible; then thoroughly wet shirt.

11. Wearing rubber gloves, mix 1 tablespoon dye powder with a little warm water in glass cup. Fill pan with enough water to cover shirt; then add dissolved dye and mix in ½ cup salt, stirring well. Add wet T-shirt to dyebath; then heat to simmering and dye for 30 minutes at that temperature.

12. At end of half-hour, remove shirt and rinse thoroughly. Wash in hot, soapy water and rinse again; allow to dry. Discard dyebath and rinse pan and cup thoroughly.

13. To remove stitching, use sharp, pointed embroidery scissors to cut off knots from one end of each thread group. Pull threads out by remaining knot, using scissor points to loosen thread. Be very careful not to cut or tear T-shirt. Press with steam iron.

SHIBORI MOTIFS

CHINESE PINE
FOLD CIRCLES IN HALF ACROSS CENTER. SEW RUNNING STITCHES ALONG EACH HALF-CIRCLE THROUGH BOTH LAYERS; MAKE STITCHES ¼" APART.

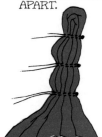

UNDULATING STRIPE
FOLD CLOTH ON LINE. SEW RUNNING STITCH ¼" FROM FOLD, WITH STITCHES ⅛" APART.

RESERVE CHEVRON
FOLD FABRIC ON LINE AND OVERCAST FOLD ¼" FROM FOLD WITH STITCHES ¼" APART; PULL CLOTH UP EVERY 5 OR 6 STITCHES.

Mayan Motif Painted Jeans

COLOR PHOTO ON PAGE 71

Turn an old pair of jeans into a bright canvas of Mayan border designs—just paint row upon row of repeat patterns with acrylic polymer paint, circling each leg and building into a series of pyramidlike steps at mid-thigh.

You'll need: 1 tube of acrylic polymer paint in *each* of the following colors: cobalt blue, medium cadmium red, light ochre, white, and purple; one 1¼″ flat and one 1⅛″ round acrylic brushes; 1 pair old flared-leg jeans (if new jeans are used, prewash before painting); old plastic dish or art palette; water soluble white marking pen; tissue paper; tracing wheel; white blackboard chalk; masking tape.

1. Enlarge and trace designs at right onto tracing paper (see page 24); then use tracing wheel to punch holes along drawn lines on tracing paper. Starting with section A, lay punched tissue paper pattern over bottom edge of right jeans leg and carefully rub blackboard chalk along punched lines to transfer design (be careful not to tear tissue paper). Move tissue along to continue design all around leg, aligning edges of pattern for complete repeat of design. If design does not match at end, make slight adjustments in pattern for correct matchup. When satisfied, trace over chalk lines with marking pen.

2. When section A has been completed, trace and mark remaining sections up right leg in this order: section B, section A, section B, section A, section B, section C, and Section D (on front of right leg). Repeat steps 1 and 2 for left leg, positioning section D on *back* of left leg.

3. Prepare and mix paints on palette or plate, using water to thin them to consistency of light cream. Starting with front of each leg, work colors one at a time to prevent bleeding into or smearing wet color areas. Allow fronts of legs to dry; then paint backs of legs.

Two applications of paint may be necessary for complete coverage since paints tend to sink into jeans fabric and darken slightly. To apply paint, refer to color key on chart for color placement (except for 2nd row of section B, where colors are reversed).

For accurate stripe widths, masking tape may be used to true up edges of stripes before painting.

4. When jeans have been completely painted, allow them to dry thoroughly; then hand wash in warm, soapy water to soften.

COLOR KEY

1	MEDIUM CADMIUM RED	4	PURPLE
2	COBALT BLUE	5	1 PART COBALT BLUE/ 1 PART PURPLE
3	LIGHT OCHRE	6	1 PART PURPLE/ 1 PART WHITE

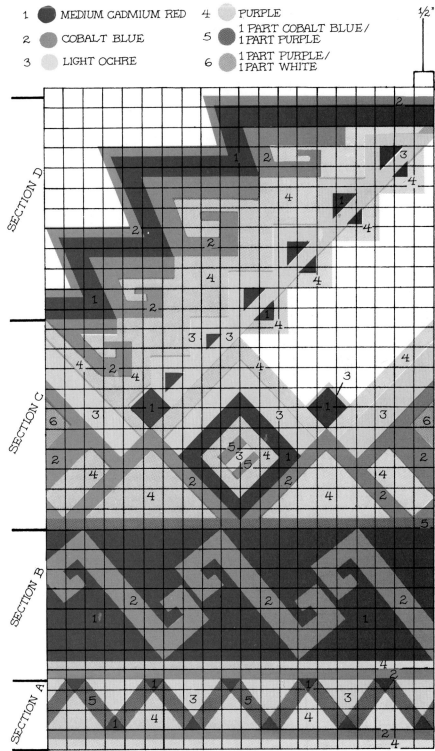

Recycling

Yarn-embroidered version of a child's drawing adds charm to an old sweater (near left). Directions are on page 75. Design: Nilda Duffek. Embroidered "keepsake" patches (far left) can be moved from shirt to shirt and added to as memories accumulate. Directions are on page 77. Design: Pat Goldstene. Knee patches made from sewing scraps (bottom, left) give new life to worn-out jeans. Directions are on page 76. Design: Lois Takaoka.

Ideas:

A. Workshirt with handbeaded yoke and rhinestone sparkled torso is a tribute to two years of dedicated stitching. Design: Patsy Lowry.

B. A fantasy collage is created when motifs cut from printed fabrics are machine appliquéd to worn jeans. Design: Linda Sampson.

A

B

Blackboard Sweater

COLOR PHOTO ON PAGE 74

Blackboard drawings have a charm all their own—trouble is, they're never permanent. We've solved that little problem, though, by transferring a child's drawing from blackboard to black sweater without losing anything in the translation except chalk dust.

An old cotton or woolen child-size turtleneck sweater can be dyed black (see page 43) for an appropriate background, then sparkled up with a pastel embroidery "drawing" of your child's (or your) favorite scene. Be sure to rinse out *all* dye after the dye bath and before beginning to embroider the sweater; if any dye remains, it will stain the pastel-colored embroidery when the sweater is washed.

You'll need: 1 ball pastel perle cotton embroidery thread (size 5) in *each* of the following colors: pistachio green (1), pale blue (2), shell pink (3), jonquil yellow (4), and white (5); small tapestry needle; construction paper or cardboard; tailor's chalk; straight pins; scissors; iron; black turtleneck child's sweater.

1. Enlarge design below and make pattern pieces from construction paper or cardboard of ship, sun, and flags. Pin or tape patterns in place on sweater and trace around them with tailor's chalk or long basting stitches. Fill in any details in the same way.

2. Using a single strand of perle cotton thread, outline shapes with stem stitching. Use sweater ribbing as a guide when working straight, vertical lines.

3. When all outlines are completed, add embroidery details on ship, flags, and sun using satin stitch, buttonhole stitch, and French knots as indicated on pattern. Add waves last; these can go completely around sweater in continuous lines. If you choose to do this, also think about adding some simple star shapes in stem stitch to back of sweater for a complete 360° design.

4. To finish, turn sweater inside out and tie any loose thread ends. Press design lightly with a warm iron. To clean sweater, wash by hand in warm, soapy water.

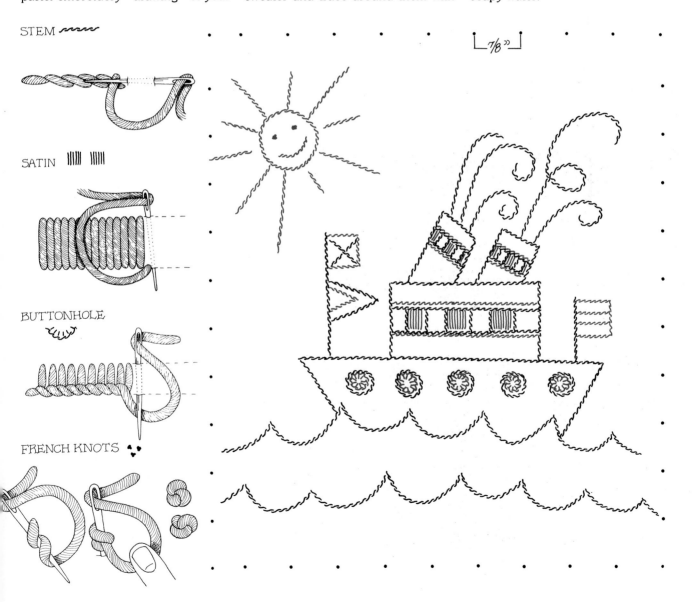

STEM

SATIN

BUTTONHOLE

FRENCH KNOTS

Scrap Knee Patches

COLOR PHOTO ON PAGE 74

If you sew, you probably have plenty of scraps around, and not just fabric scraps either. We'll show you how ribbons, threads, and trims can be put to good use.

The "city" and "desert" patches on these jeans were whipped up on the sewing machine from assorted scraps, then appliquéd to the jeans by hand. For comfort and durability, old potholders could be tucked behind each knee patch for extra padding.

You'll need: Scraps of cotton fabric in the following sizes and colors: two 7 by 7″ gold, one 4 by 4″ yellow, one 8 by 8″ orange and green striped, one 2 by 8″ orange, one 7 by 7″ white, one 7 by 3″ beige, and one 7 by 3″ dark green; one red iron-on patch; 1 spool cotton thread in *each* of the following colors: yellow, orange, gold, green, blue, and black; 8 black hook eyes and 24 black hook loops; waterproof black marking pen; 1 pr. 40″-long black shoelaces; 1 skein orange cotton embroidery thread; 2 small red

ball-shaped buttons; zigzag sewing machine.

1. Enlarge patterns below (see page 24) and transfer to gold background fabric; then cut patterns apart to serve as guides for cutting appliqués.

2. Cut appliqué pieces from appropriate fabrics, following shaped edges exactly, but adding ½″ for seams to all overlapped and outside edges of squares (fig. 76-A).

3. For "city" patch, use original pattern as placement guide for appliqués. First, topstitch buildings along upper edge; then position greenery over bottom of buildings and sew along curving edge of greenery with 4 parallel rows of green and blue machine zigzag stitching. For bushes, add curved rows of zigzag stitching as indicated on pattern.

4. Adjacent to bottom edge of greenery, sew down 7 by 3″ piece of beige fabric along top edge.

5. Using orange thread, topstitch along both edges of 1 strip of orange fabric placed over butted edges of greenery and beige fabric.

6. Cut car from iron-on patch and draw in details with marking pen. Iron car to beige fabric area.

7. Draw windows on buildings with marking pen; then use figure 76-B as guide for sewing hook loops and eyes to orange strip for iron fence effect.

8. Trim ends from 1 shoelace. Top-

stitch lacing over raw upper edge of building appliqué, making corners and turns as in figure 76-C. Set aside.

9. To make "desert" patch, use original pattern as placement and cutting guide. Cut a 2½″-diameter circle of yellow fabric, and a 4¼ by 7″ rectangle of orange and green striped fabric (cut on the diagonal); tear 2 by 8″ piece of orange fabric in half lengthwise. Position sun at upper center of gold fabric background; machine zigzag into place. Add 9 overlapping rows of orange and yellow machine zigzag around sun for halo.

10. Tear a strip roughly ½ by 4″ from yellow fabric. Topstitch several times with yellow thread over sun and gold background.

11. Torn edge up, topstitch 1 by 8″ strip of orange fabric (see step 9) over lower edge of sun.

12. Fold under top edge of diagonally striped rectangle and position over lower edge of orange strip; secure rectangle in place with 3 rows of orange topstitching.

13. Cut out and topstitch cacti into place; draw thorns with marking pen. Trim ends from remaining shoelace and topstitch over edges of cacti.

14. Sew red buttons onto cacti.

15. To attach patches to jeans, turn under ½″ on all edges and iron. Pin patches in place at knees. Blanket stitch patches (fig. 76-D) in place with 2 strands of orange embroidery floss.

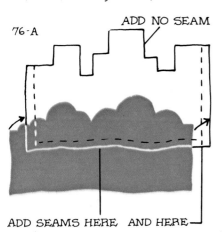

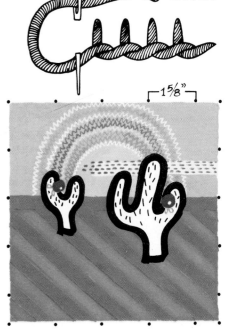

Keepsake Patches

COLOR PHOTO ON PAGE 74

As the song says, we all have our "favorite things" . . . and what better way to carry them with us through the years than keepsake patches? To begin your child's collection, here are eight pictures of favorite things to be embroidered, and then appliquéd to an existing shirt.

As time passes, add more keepsake patches until you have a whole collection. When the shirt wears out, simply remove the patches and sew them to a new garment. Two of the embroidery stitches used—split stitch and couching—are illustrated below;

illustrations for remaining stitches are on page 26.

You'll need: 1 skein cotton embroidery floss in *each* of the following colors: black (1), light grey (2), dark grey (3), light brown (4), dark brown (5), beige (6), light blue (7), medium blue (8), dark blue (9), medium green (10), gold (11), yellow (12), orange (13), pink (14), red (15), purple (16), and white (17); crewel embroidery needle; medium-size embroidery hoop; scissors; pencil; pins; iron; ¼ yard cotton homespun fabric in *each* of the following colors: khaki, pale blue, and rust; 1 spool cotton thread in *each* of the following colors: khaki, pale blue, and rust.

1. Enlarge patterns below and transfer to appropriate cloth background (see photo on page 74). Space patterns out on fabric with several inches between them. This leaves room for background and seam allowances on all pieces and makes use of an embroidery hoop easier. *Do not* cut out individual patches yet.

2. Divide all embroidery floss into 2-strand segments.

3. Fit fabric into embroidery hoop, centering entire design to be worked and keeping fabric taut. Begin embroidering outlines of design; then go on to solid areas. Progress from 1 color to another, following color and stitch guides given below.

4. When embroidery is completed, lay fabric flat. Using a ruler as a guide, lightly draw outlines for each patch around embroidered design with pencil. Draw a 2nd line ⅝″ outside 1st outline for seam allowances.

5. Cut out each patch along outside line. Fold seams under; iron flat.

6. Pin patches on shirt and slipstitch with matching thread.

STITCH GUIDE

COUCHING

SPLIT

SLIP

DOT-TO-DOT OWL
BRANCH: CHAIN
PENCIL LINE:
COUCHING/LEAVES: RANDOM/DOTS:
FRENCH KNOTS/EYES & FEATHERS:
SPLIT/NUMBERS: BACKSTITCH

ENVELOPE
OUTLINE: CHAIN/STAMP: SPLIT
ADDRESS & CANCELLATION: BACKSTITCH

PUZZLE
WATER & SAILS: CHAIN/FLAG & BOAT:
SATIN/MAST: HEAVY CHAIN/LINES
OF PUZZLE: BACKSTITCH

GUMBALL MACHINE
GUMBALLS: SATIN/GLASS DOME:
HEAVY CHAIN/MACHINE BODY: CHAIN

FLY (2 STRANDS OF FLOSS THROUGHOUT)
BODY & WINGS: SATIN/ANTENNAE &
LEGS: BACKSTITCH/EYES: CLUSTERS
OF FRENCH KNOTS

CRAYON
CRAYON & PAPER: SATIN
LABEL: BACKSTITCH

PENCIL
PENCIL & POINT: SATIN

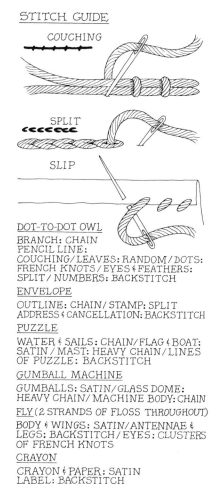

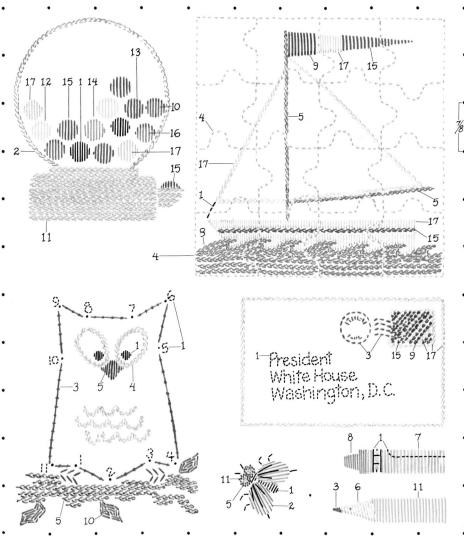

Supply List
Bibliography

Suppliers

Fabrics, Notions, Leather

Imported silks and cottons—Exotic Thai Silks, 393 Main, Los Altos, CA 94022

Domestic and imported fabrics and notions—Fibers, Ghirardelli Square, San Francisco, CA 94109

Imported hand-woven fabrics—Handloomed Fabric Store, 1502 Walnut Street, Berkeley, CA 94709

Japanese ikat, tie-dye, and print fabrics—Kasuri Dyeworks, 1959 Shattuck Avenue, Berkeley, CA 94704

Old English country floral cottons—Laura Ashley Inc., 735 Montgomery Street, San Francisco, CA 94111

Fabrics for dyes and paints—Test Fabrics, P.O. Box Drawer "O", 200 Blackford Avenue, Middlesex, NJ 08846

Trims and notions—Handcrafts of Europe, P.O. Box 372, Sausalito, CA 94965

Ethnic garment patterns—Folkwear Ethnic Patterns, P.O. Box 98, Forestville, CA 95436

Russian Punchneedle—Igolochkoy, P.O. Box 818, Dept. 27, Palo Alto, CA 94302

Machine embroidery thread, yarns, beads—Folklorico Yarn Company, 526 Ramona Street, Palo Alto, CA 94301

Feathers, shells, beads, yarn—Naturalcraft, 2199 Bancroft Way, Berkeley, CA 94704

Leather and supplies—C. T. Struven, 23 Joseph Court, San Rafael, CA 94903

Dye, Paint, and Silkscreen Supplies

Dyes, paints, batik supplies, fabrics—Dharma Trading Company, P.O. Box 915, San Rafael, CA 94901

Dyes, paints, printing and batik supplies—Cerulean Blue, 1314 N.E. 43rd Street, Seattle, WA 98105

Dyes, paints, stencil and batik supplies—Aiko's Art Materials, 714 North Wabash Avenue, Chicago, IL 60611

Dyes—Fezandie and Sperrle, Inc., 103 Lafayette Street, New York, NY 10013

Textile paint in tubes—Tri Chem Inc., 1 Cape May Street, Harrison, NJ 07029

Oil-base paints, stencil paper, equipment—Prang Textile Colors, American Crayon Co., Sandusky, OH 44870

Vat dyes, silkscreen products—Screen Process Supplies Mfg. Co., 1199 East 12 Street, Oakland, CA 94606

Silkscreen products—California Process Supply Co., 3836 10 Street, Berkeley, CA 94710

Liquid textile resist for hot dyebaths—Polyproducts Corp., 13810 Nelson Avenue, Detroit, MI 48227

Bibliography

Clothing Construction

Burnham, Dorthy. *Cut My Cote*. Toronto: Royal Ontario Museum, 1973.

Calasibetta, Dr. Charlotte. *Fairchild's Dictionary of Fashion*. New York: Fairchild Publications, 1975.

Clabburn, Pamela. *Needleworker's Dictionary*. New York: Morrow, 1976.

_____. *Art of Sewing* Series. New York: Time-Life, 1973.

Historical Costume Sources

Houston, Mary G. *Ancient Egyptian, Mesopotamian, and Persian Costume and Decoration*. New York: Harper and Row, 1954.

Lipman, Jean, and Winchester, Alice. *The Flowering of American Folk Art*. New York: Viking Press, 1974.

Priest, Alan. *Costumes from the Forbidden City*. New York: Arno Press, 1972.

Tilke, Max. *Costume Patterns and Designs*. Philadelphia: Hastings House, 1974.

Tilke, Max and Bruhn, W. *Pictorial History of Costume*. Philadelphia: Hastings House, 1976.

Costume as Social Change

Jacopetti, Alexandra, and Wainwright, Jerry. *Native Funk and Flash*. San Francisco: Scrimshaw Press, 1974.

Laury, Jean Ray, and Aiken, Joyce. *Creating Body Coverings*. New York: Van Nostrand Reinhold, 1973.

Milinaire, Caterine, and Troy, Carol. *Cheap Chic*. New York: Harmony Books, 1975.

Rudofsky, Bernard. *The Unfashionable Human Body*. New York: Doubleday, 1974.

Squire, Geoffrey. *Dress and Society 1560—1970*. New York: Viking Press, 1974.

Wolman, Baron. *Levi's Denim Art Contest Catalogue of Winners*. Mill Valley, CA: Square Books, 1974.

Decorations and Techniques

Auld, Rhoda L. *Molas*. New York: Van Nostrand Reinhold, 1976.

Auvil, Kenneth W. *Serigraphy: Silk Screen Techniques for the Artist*. Englewood Cliffs, NJ: Prentice-Hall, 1965.

Bakke, Karen. *The Sewing Machine as a Creative Tool*. Englewood Cliffs, NJ: Prentice-Hall, 1976.

D'Harcourt, Raoul. *Textiles of Ancient Peru and Their Techniques*. Seattle: University of Washington Press, 1974.

_____. *Dover Pictorial Archives* Series. New York: Dover Publications.

Edson, Nicki, and Stimmel, Arlene. *Creative Crochet*. New York: Watson-Guptil, 1973.

Fanning, Roberta. *Decorative Machine Stitchery*. New York: Butterick Publishing Co., 1976.

Gutcheon, Beth. *The Perfect Patchwork Primer*. New York: McKay, 1973.

Houston, John. *Batik with Neil Dyrenforth*. New York: Bobbs-Merrill, 1976.

Howard, Constance. *Embroidery and Color*. New York: Van Nostrand Reinhold, 1976.

Karasz, Mariska. *Adventures in Stitches*. New York: Funk & Wagnalls, 1975.

Lubell, Cecil. *Textile Collections of the World* Series. New York: Van Nostrand Reinhold, 1976.

Meilach, Dona. *Contemporary Batik and Tie Dye*. New York: Crown, 1973.

Sieber, Roy. *African Textiles and Decorative Arts*. New York: Museum of Modern Art, 1972.

Valentino, Richard, and Mufson, Phyllis. *Fabric Printing: Screen Method*. San Francisco: Bay Books, 1975.

Wilson, Erica. *Erica Wilson's Embroidery Book*. New York: Charles Scribner and Sons, 1973.

Wilson, Jean. *Weaving You Can Wear*. New York: Van Nostrand Reinhold, 1973.

Recycling

Brock, Delia, and Bodger, Lorraine. *Glad Rags*. New York: Simon and Schuster, 1974.

Funario, Diana. *Yestermorrow Clothesbook*. Radmor, PA: Chilton, 1976.

Ideas: Witty and Whimsical

A

B

There's a certain amount of pleasure derived from keeping your creative tongue in cheek while working with fabrics, floss, paints, and knitting needles. A healthy sense of humor keeps clothing decorators from taking themselves too seriously, as you can see from the examples shown at right and below. Try your hand at cracking a visual joke or at making a nonverbal pun. It's fun! For more creative ideas, see pages 16, 17, 40, 41, 56, and 57.

A. A trio of brickstitch-embroidered cows meanders across the front yoke of a crisp blue workshirt. Design: Megan Rickards.

B. Class instructor's keepsake workshirt is covered with pockets, each decorated with love and humor by a grateful former student. Design: Students of Roberta Horton, Berkeley.

C. "Clint's Ceremonial Shirt" swims with mandalas, mushrooms, flames, and feathers drawn with waterproof felt markers on washable cotton velvet. Design: Beth Pewther.

D. Whimsical hand-knit "Circus Sweater" includes yarn embroidery and spool-knitted performers sewn to the finished sweater. Design: Amy Bahrt.

C

D

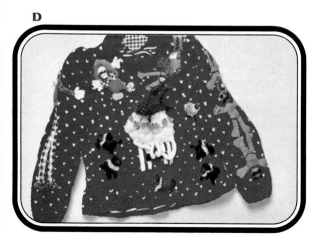

Index

Photographers

All photographs in this book are by Jerry Wainwright except as follows: Franklin Avery, 40-C; Irv Bahrt, 79-D; Renato P. Bartoli, 25 inset; Roger Buchanan, 56-D, 74-A; Maria de Conceição, 68 left; Marika Contompasis, 40-A, 68 right; Jean Cook, 17-H; Charles Decker, 5-D, 59 inset; Fiberworks, 17-M; Karen B. Foster, 39-B; Mona Helcermanas-Benge, 16-B, 16-C, 16-E, 17-J, 17-L, 17-O; Julia Hill, 57-K; Chris Hodenfield, 41-I; Demetre Lagios, 56-A; Carolyn Oberst, 57-I; Jessica Overstreet, 41-H; Marion Patterson, 57-H; Beth M. Pewther, 79-C; Burdette A. Pickett, 40-E; Yvonne Porcella, 5-C; Megan Rickards, 79-A; Cindy Sägen, 16-A, 16-D, 17-K, 17-N, 17-P; Linda Sampson, 74-B; Deborah Slabeck, 51 inset; Sunshine, 41-J; Allan Tannenbaum, 1-A, 5-E; The Philadelphia Gallery, 57-G; Steve Thurston, 40-D; Susan Wick, 18-B; Linda Witt, 41-F.